Meeting
the Needs
of the
Retarded

MEETING THE NEEDS OF THE RETARDED

A critical look at current approaches

by Robert Isaacson, Ph.D

Argus Communications
Niles, Illinois

ARGUS COMMUNICATIONS
7440 Natchez Avenue
Niles, Illinois 60648

International Standard Book Number 0-913592-94-3
Library of Congress Number 77-90137

1 2 3 4 5 6 7 8 9 0

To Mary Ingrid and her friends

CONTENTS

Dr. Robert Isaacson is a professor of psychology at the University of Florida. He is also the parent of a retarded person. But, above all, he is a compassionate realist.

In this compact book, Dr. Isaacson shatters myths that many sincere but misguided people hold about mental deficiency. He substitutes, instead, realistic facts about the true abilities, limitations, and needs of the retarded adult.

Then, he proceeds to outline the kinds of programs, services, and living conditions that are necessary to allow for maximum happiness and personal growth for these individuals.

Dr. Isaacson offers all of us a clear middle-of-the road perspective on what we can do to enhance life for thousands of mentally handicapped people. He effectively scraps extreme views at both ends of the spectrum—those who act as if the mentally deficient can and should be totally "normalized" and those who would wrap the retarded in swaddling clothes and treat them like infants all of their days. Instead he asks for understanding and acceptance based on fact, dignity, and respect.

As President of the Mental Retardation Association of America, I am grateful to Dr. Isaacson for so effectively presenting a sensible outline for meeting the needs of these very special people. His views are in total harmony with the purposes of our national organization.

Senator Ernest H. Dean, Utah State Senate
President, Mental Retardation Association
of America, Inc.

In highly readable, almost conversational style, psychologist Robert Isaacson states his positions on many issues concerning mental deficiency without equivocation in this new book on retardation. This concise book certainly fits the man as I have known him in Florida—a forthright, plain-spoken advocate for the mentally deficient.

A long-time student of retardation, as well as father of a retarded daughter, this eminent neurobiologist pulls no punches in looking at the present "state of the art." He attacks as misguided those who view the retarded as "perpetual children" or persons living in a "different culture" from the one most of us know. He uses his verbal sword freely in reference to the present-day emphasis on "normalization" and deinstitutionalization.

Both, according to Isaacson, are too often predicated on the basis of saving money. The popular movement among administrators accountable to state legislators is to reduce institution populations, moving as many persons as possible to "more normal" living situations in the community. Yet, writes Isaacson, the parents have reason to be concerned. He points out that, while a particular group home in the community and its house parents may seem "nice," parents must be concerned about the long-term prospects their children face. To many retarded individuals released to community group homes later end up in dire circumstances.

Isaacson speaks freely of sex and the retarded. His solution calls for consensus and then commitment on the part of parents and staff regarding the subject matter that must be presented.

In Isaacson's opinion, psychotherapy and reality therapy are not suitable treatment approaches for the retarded. While behavior modification has proven advantages, a "humanistic" approach is what he favors. By this, he means that the retarded should be looked upon as "guests" in our society. Afflicted with a permanent handicap that sets them apart, most cannot be molded into middle-class Americans through better or earlier training. Instead of a ceaseless effort, therefore, to make them more productive, we should concentrate on allowing them greater freedom of choice and dignity wherever they are. If they wish to move to a community residence, fine! And, if they feel more comfortable in moving back to an institution later, that's fine, too. Wherever they live, retarded persons should find attractive, humane living conditions. The clean, well-kept wards should not be used only for those with the "greatest promise."

Since so many of us think in terms of "the bottom line," Isaacson points out that a humanistic approach to working with retarded persons will certainly be no more costly than our present practices. With greater freedom to live in apartments or group homes under conditions they have some voice in determining, staff supervision can be reduced. *There is no reason why such living arrangements cannot be established on the grounds of existing institutions.*

For parents, administrators, and those with concern for persons with this serious handicap, Isaacson writes plainly and clearly, making definite recommendations on how retarded persons can be treated, both more fairly and more wisely.

O. J. Keller, Former Secretary,
Department of Health and Rehabilitative Services,
State of Florida

A few years ago, I tried to describe the significance of having a retarded child from the point of view of a parent. No doubt it was influenced by my perspective as a professional psychologist. The result was *The Retarded Child* (Argus, 1974). In it I tried to provide an awareness of what can be expected when a retarded child is born in terms of the reactions of each parent, the changes in relationships between the parents, and among the parents and their friends. Furthermore, I tried to suggest ways in which the difficult decisions facing the parents could be made, based on a realistic evaluation of available options.

Since the publication of that book, my life has been changed by my involvement with The Regional Human Rights Advocacy Committees for the Mentally Retarded and with two temporary state-wide committees working on programs for the mentally handicapped, and by watching my own retarded daughter grow into her teens. Slowly, I began to realize that neither she, nor any other mentally deficient individual, had been viewed in what I consider to be the most appropriate perspectives: First, as a different biological being than most people, and second, as an individual for whom many personal rewards and joys were possible, provided society looked at her and her friends somewhat differently. Over time, I came to realize that my own biological background could provide the basis of a behavioral philosophy or ethic. More important, I came to recognize the great value of approaching the topic of mental deficiency from the point of view of a "humanist," a person who values personal freedom, growth, and love beyond all else.

Using biological and humanistic principles, a new approach to life for the mentally deficient could be achieved. Certainly, my friend, the late Sidney Jourard, planted the seeds from which these ideas flowered but they were well-nourished by my wife and friend, Ann Braden, and by my close associates at the University of Florida, especially Dr. Carol Van Hartesveldt. I appreciate their advice on this manuscript as on so many professional matters. I would also like to thank the following people who gave me helpful comments on earlier drafts of the manuscript: Dr. Lawson Crowe, Behavior Genetics Institute at the University of Colorado; Mr. Max Hutt, psychologist and co-author with me of two textbooks in the field of psychology, Ann Arbor, Michigan; Mr. O. J. Keller, now at the University of Florida, formerly Secretary, Department of Health and Rehabilitative Services, State of Florida; Dr. Ted Landsman, Professor of Psychology, University of Florida; Ms. Cordelia McClelland, Director, Sunshine School, Gainesville, Florida; Mr. Robert Perry, Director, Annandale Village, Georgia; and Ms. Cissy Ross, reporter, *The Gainesville Sun*. Finally, I would like to express my appreciation to my secretary, Mrs. Virginia Walker, who for 10 years now has helped me so much on so many different projects and programs.

Robert L. Isaacson

ONE

The People and Their Problems

Most mentally retarded children grow up to become adults. Perhaps not quite as many of them do make it into adulthood as do their nonretarded contemporaries, for along with their intellectual problems the mentally retarded often have physical abnormalities that cut their lives short. Heart defects, respiratory disorders, seizures, and a host of similar ailments take their toll of the mentally handicapped. But the fact remains; most of them do become adults.

Yet our attention has been chiefly devoted to retarded children. It is for them that our hearts and pocketbooks are opened. Advertising campaigns, human interest stories, and fund drives all are directed toward the retarded child. What happens as the child grows up? What sort of life does the retarded live then? What can and should be done for the retarded adult?

Thinking about the lives of retarded adults is not a popular occupation. Retarded adults have lost the attractive qualities associated with children. The magic of the early growth period has vanished and been replaced with the less dramatic, static condition of the more or less completed person. Gone, too, are the hopes of childhood. With a child it is always possible to hope and pray that through training, drugs, life experience, or just plain growing up, the mental handicaps of the child will

2

fade. When adulthood is reached, the hopes have proved empty, the prayers have gone unanswered.

The *mentally retarded* child or adult is really misnamed. The term *retarded* implies a falling behind in development that is misleading, in that it gives rise to false hopes. If growth is only retarded, there is the chance of catching up. For most of the mentally handicapped this catching up is *not* going to occur. The biological conditions that caused the mental deficiencies will not allow it. It is better to face the problem squarely from the start. The term *mental deficiency* should be used to describe the handicaps of both children and adults that result from severe and early brain damage. In the past, other terms have been used to describe the mentally handicapped, including imbecile, idiot, and moron. These have been dropped from current usage, because they were so frequently used derisively to belittle the individuals involved. They have been replaced by terms denoting various degrees of mental deficiency or retardation: the *profoundly* deficient (retarded), the *severely* deficient (retarded), the *mildly* or *moderately* deficient (retarded). Various other terms are also used: educable, trainable, high level, low level. However, even these terms can be used to belittle. Within an institution employees and some residents often describe other residents as high or low grade (relatively bright or dull, respectively). But, whatever terms are used, they should represent people as having a *permanent handicap* but not making a judgment about their value.

An individual suffering from some degree of mental deficiency is less able than others not so afflicted to cope with his or her environment and with society. He or she is less fit when viewed in terms of chances for personal survival and the perpetuation of the species, but this should not be interpreted as the person being any less human or worthy of our consideration. The biological events responsible for mental deficiencies are neither good nor bad in and of themselves. They are simply blind biological events.

The Lives of the Mentally Deficient

Mental deficiency is not adequately described by any set of test scores or any other existing forms of mental measurement. It is best described as a serious inability to deal with the problems presented to the individual by his family, culture, and society. This inability to deal with the environment is a consequence of a brain which is not capable of performing the functions needed to make an independent life possible. Substantial per-

4

sonal assistance is needed. Life itself could not be sustained without the continuing support of other people. A few examples demonstrate this.

Charlie is a twenty-five-year-old man who helps collect trash and garbage in a large institution for the mentally deficient. He wears a big grin most of the day and wears a dog-eared hat which once was red but now is almost colorless. Charlie loves his hat, his friends who room with him in a twenty-man cottage, and even the trash truck that takes him and three other residents of the institution on their daily rounds. In the morning Charlie starts each day in fresh, clean clothes, but by four in the afternoon the day's work has left its marks and odors on him. Charlie, his clothes, and his beloved hat are wilted.

When I first talked with Charlie it was after four PM. He is a slight man with a face that is a bit lopsided. A friend introduced us. We shook hands.

"How are you, Charlie?" I asked.

"Uyg, see-ug." was the reply.

"See-ug?" I asked.

Charlie pointed at the package of cigarettes he had seen in my shirt pocket.

"Oh, cigarette! You want a cigarette?"

"Yuh, see-ut-et," Charlie said.

Charlie lit up the cigarette I gave him, and stretched out in his chair with his hands folded behind his head. His legs were extended straight out, the feet crossed at the ankles.

"Do you know Mr._____who takes care of the truck?" I asked.

"Yuh."

"Do you like your job?"

(No reply)

"What don't you like about it?"

(No reply)

"Do you like the money you get?"

"Yuh."

"Do you get paid enough?"

"Yuh."

In the next fifteen minutes or so I found that Charlie could say more than "yuh" and its negative, "huh." Sounds representing cigarettes, matches, truck, trash, were available to him, and he understood a good deal more than he could say. If I used long sentences and unfamiliar words, however, his attention lapsed. He looked out the window, studied his cigarette, or stared at nothing in particular, his eyes seemingly focused on something several miles away.

I tried to find out what Charlie would do if he got more money from his job. Cigarettes and candy were priority items but the main thing was, apparently, the fact that Charlie needed money to buy small presents for a girl friend.

I talked with Charlie's co-worker, George. Both worked on the trash truck. George was older, in his mid-thirties, and had a round pudgy face, prominent but not harsh features, and a vast number of pock marks.

He was dressed neatly in overalls and a red checkered shirt. He smiled a great deal and when he did his pumpkinlike face lit up. Somehow he seemed to be less soiled than Charlie, although both had the same sort of job.

"How are you, George?"

"Fine, fine."

"Enjoy your job?"

"Sure, who's dat?" George pointed at a picture of a ten-year-old girl on the wall. I told him and asked,

"Do you know Charlie?"

"Sure, sure, fine boy."

"Do you make enough money?"

"Sure, sure. What's dat?"

George pointed at a plaque on another part of the wall. I explained the plaque. George beamed.

"Do you get paid enough?"

"Fine, fine, what's dat?"

Now George was pointing to another picture farther along the wall.

"Lemme see."

I took down the picture and handed it to him. He studied it carefully.

"Dot-ter?"

"Yes, George, it is Mr._____'s daughter."

"Fine."

I soon gave up trying to find out about George's feelings about his job or his supervisors. He said "fine" and "sure" in response to every question, only occasionally amplifying his remarks. Even two consecutive, contradictory questions would be answered affirmatively. George scanned the room incessantly and asked about everything. After being told about a picture or an object, he would usually produce a one-word response.

These two men are not mentally retarded, they are mentally deficient. They will not grow out of their problems. Despite their past training by speech therapists, they still have serious language problems. Additional speech therapy might help these men to communicate a bit more effectively, but even this is doubtful.

These young men were working at jobs that were of value to their community. In their case the community was the institution. Their deficiencies did not preclude their making tangible contributions to the lives of others through their sweat and toil. Furthermore, these men liked what they were doing. They liked the trash truck. They enjoyed their own jokes, and had fun with each other and with other people on the grounds of the institution. They had room and board, medical and dental care. The small amount of money they earned was adequate to provide for some small luxuries. They were in a highly structured and protective environment. However, their lives could be better. More joys, freedoms, and opportunities could be available to them. (Suggestions about how this could be done will be given in Chapter 6.) It should be noted, nevertheless, that with their abilities and skills life outside the institution would only be possible with close supervision.

Community Living

Jane is twenty-two years old and lives in a group-living home supported by the state. There are fourteen other women in the home. For most of her life she lived at home, but when her parents' age and health made it almost impossible to care for her, she was placed in an institution. Less than two years after being placed there, she was transferred to the group-living home.

Her speech is relatively good. She can communicate her thoughts and ideas clearly, although bluntly, in a slow, telegraphic fashion. Her sentences contain but a few words and are always simple and direct. Jane's day starts early, about six AM, being awakened by the alarm clock set by the home operator the night before. Jane cannot tell time, although she wears a wrist watch to be like other people. After washing up, she goes to the kitchen and on most days pours out milk and cereal for herself, although sometimes another girl will cook eggs for everyone. About seven-thirty AM, the group home operator drives Jane and two other girls to a nearby motel where they work the next eight hours as maids, changing linens, mopping, and cleaning. Then, the motel's station wagon drives the girls home.

Jane likes to be home by three PM to watch the afternoon soap operas and game shows on television. On some afternoons, young volunteer workers from the community come over and try to get her to join the others in volley ball or other yard games, but they have to force Jane to play. She resents being taken away from her television. On two nights each week, all of the women get together and talk about what they are doing and how they are getting along. These sessions are led by a social worker paid by the state. Jane loves the sessions because she is able to talk fairly well and has become sort of a leader in the discussions. She likes most of the women who live with her, although there are a few that she does not get along with. When asked why she does not like these few, she only says they are "no good," or "bad." Some other residents in the home feel that Jane is "stuck up."

On paydays a social worker takes Jane to the bank and then out shopping with some of her leftover funds. Jane does not understand making change and money is measured only by "little" or "lots." If left on her own, Jane would spend all she has on whatever strikes her fancy. She buys trinkets and bright things and loves to give them away to her friends.

Jane resists depositing any money in the bank but has become resigned to it. Why she should give money to a bank teller is a great mystery to her.

Jane says she is happy but would be happier without the "bad girls" in the home. She loves to watch television

and attend the evening discussions. She
would like to have a boy friend but
does not know how to find one. She
likes to attend movies, picnics, and go on
the trips that are sometimes arranged
for the girls. Her life is productive
but less than ideal. She too would like
more freedom, but is afraid of it.
She feels safe in the home. She is not
tempted to leave it except with her
social worker or with other residents
in a large group.

These are examples of success stories, even
though the degree of success is modest by
most standards. Other stories of failure could
be told. For example, one of the women
living at the group home with Jane is fairly
attractive. Some male employees of the
motel found that she was willing to have
sexual intercourse with them at any time.
They also found that she was willing to visit
guests and have sexual relations with them.
The employees charged the guests for providing the girl, and she became a prostitute
for them, at least until they were arrested.

Not all men in institutions are as happy as
Charlie and George. Some mentally deficient
men like these two do get enjoyment from
their work. Some do not work at all but spend
their days going to and from the mess hall,
watching television, or doing nothing. Some

mentally deficient people with physical problems spend their days in bed with nothing at all to occupy their time.

In all cultures, mentally deficient people have problems surviving. Unfortunately, very little is known of the lives of such individuals beyond the limits of modern industrial societies, but what has been recorded by visitors to isolated cultures suggests the mentally deficient person to be at a disadvantage no matter how simple life seems to be.

Farley Mowat describes the life of one "dull-witted" Eskimo in his book *People of the Deer.** This man could not master hunting despite continued attempts and never was able to kill a single deer during the time of Mowat's visit to the inland Eskimos of northern Canada. This handicap could easily have been fatal, since the hunter must kill deer for food, clothes, and almost all of the necessities of life for himself and his family. They survived only because other hunters provided the deer for the deficient Eskimo and his family. In return the dull-witted Eskimo provided a source of amusement to the others and seemed to enjoy his special role as an unwitting jester.

---

*Mowat, F. *People of the Deer*, Boston: Little-Brown, 1952.

The mentally deficient Eskimo was maintained by the efforts of friends and relatives around him. From Mowat's description, it can be inferred that he was mildly or moderately deficient. The fate of a more deficient person would be less certain despite the charity and good humor of the inland Eskimos. Relatively few Eskimo children survive the first few years of life and the physical handicaps of the more profoundly deficient would surely lead to early death. Furthermore, the rigors of life in the Northland are so great that a stern set of priorities is imposed for the distribution of food during times of famine. The hunter must be fed first. He must be kept alive for without him the others must surely die. The second priority is a fecund wife from whom future life arises. Third, are those with new life: the children. Lowest on the priorities of life in times of hardships are those who cannot hunt to provide food or provide new life: the aged and infirm. It is likely that Mowat's dull-witted incompetent hunter would be classified with the latter in bad times and sacrificed in some more or less gentle fashion when food supplies became desperately short.

All people with a substantial mental handicap must depend on the help of others for direction, guidance, and the essentials required to deal with the culture. Without this help they could not survive. It is a matter of life and death.

The Mentally Deficient in Modern Society

The mildly or moderately deficient person in our society has three fundamental problems. These are time, money, and planning for the future. Much of modern life depends on the understanding of time and money. Even the simple act of setting an alarm clock is important since most employers expect some degree of promptness in their employees. Making change and budgeting limited financial resources are critical to getting along in the modern world. Just as critical is the need to understand the reasons for saving money, buying licenses, purchasing insurance, getting medical and dental evaluations, and the use of modern appliances. These are a few of the complexities of life with which the moderately mentally deficient person has the greatest problems and with which help is needed.

The severely and profoundly retarded must be given even greater care and supervision, so much so that many need the care and protection of an institution. Their needs are of a more fundamental nature, and therefore plans for their lives must differ from those for the moderately and mildly deficient.

Reactions to the Mentally Deficient

What do people think about the mentally deficient? How do they react to them? What do they think should be done for them? While these are questions of interest, a more pertinent question is how *should* society think about and act toward the mentally deficient? The answer that mentally deficient people should be treated in the same ways as everyone else is too simple. It just will not do.

The way we treat another person depends on how we value them. Indeed, any interaction between two people depends on how each sees the other. Hitler saw the Jews, Slavs, and other non-Aryans as worthless, despicable, less-than-human. The slave owner and the Klansman saw blacks as inferior products of nature. There is an additional step beyond thinking of people as inferior: thinking of people as inanimate objects that can be manipulated, like chess pieces, or thrown away like crumpled pieces of waste paper.

It is not uncommon for the mentally deficient to be treated indeed as objects. I have heard mildly mentally deficient people described as objects to be moved or otherwise treated without regard to their individual concerns, abilities, or desires. It reminds me of the orders that Adolf Eichmann issued for Jews to be transported to Treblinka.

16

Differences in appearance, life-styles, and customs all serve as potential bases of differentiation among people. When someone looks or acts differently, the person is not one of "us," and we almost automatically devalue them. *We* are better and *they* are worse because they wear hats when we do not, or they have a different color of skin, or they just look different. Since many mentally deficient people *do* look and act differently, we tend to make a low evaluation of them from the start. It is perhaps surprising that the mentally deficient are as well received by society as they are.

A recent poll commissioned by the President's Committee on Mental Retardation provided information about how well the American public accepts those with mental deficiencies. A considerable majority of Americans would not object to a small number of mentally deficient people living in a group home on their block or to having a mentally deficient person employed where they work. Most of those interviewed believed that some percentage could manage to live outside of institutions. About half of those interviewed believed that most of the mentally deficient cannot support themselves and lead independent lives. One out of every seven people in the poll considered the mentally deficient person to be dangerous. In summary, Americans seem to have a rather complex and mixed attitude toward the mentally handicapped. On the one hand, they seem to think that many could survive outside of institutions and lead more-or-less independent lives. Yet, there is strong current of feeling that extended care and supervision will be required. There is a segment of the population that believes that society must protect itself from the mentally deficient who could be dangerous. Most feel that a limited association with the mentally deficient is acceptable but do not relish prolonged or frequent contact.

How accurate are these judgments? Can most of the mentally deficient really lead lives of reasonable quality and hold jobs competitively as is sometimes advocated? Can they be assimilated into society?

I think that the popular views expressed in the poll are overly optimistic in regard to the capabilities held by most mentally deficient people. We have been led to think that the vast majority of the mentally handicapped can be trained and educated to the point where they can live and work on their own. Actually, supervision, care, and guidance will be necessary for most. The greater the handicap the more the supervision that will be needed. What must be done is to consider the nature of each person's handicap and then to

18

provide ways in which the individual can live most profitably and productively given his or her limitations.

Still More

Many mentally deficient people suffer from physical and emotional handicaps, as well. By some estimates about sixty percent of the mentally handicapped living in institutions suffer from some form of convulsions. Epileptic disorders can be of several different forms and not all are controlled by medication.

Other mentally deficient people suffer from cerebral palsy, that is, those disorders of the brain that affect the musculature and movements of the body. Arms and legs may be pulled in toward the body and distorted into unusual postures. Many mentally deficient people have very little muscle tone at best, and a general awkwardness in their actions.

While far from being a general rule, often mentally deficient people are less attractive physically than those with more usual abilities. This can be due to physical deformities or other reasons, including a lack of interest in their appearance. It is often the case that they receive less training in how to make themselves attractive.

All of these factors work together to produce an individual who is less likely to do well in the world, without even taking into account the mental deficiency itself. An awkward, uncoordinated, seizure-prone, and unattractive person would not be sought as an employee even if he or she had normal mental abilities.

As if these problems were not enough, the mentally deficient person is beset with emotional problems, as well. Some psychiatrists and psychologists believe that almost all mentally deficient people—children and adults—suffer some form of emotional disorder, while other, more cautious observers say only that emotional problems are more frequently found among the mentally deficient than among the nondeficient. Of course, it is often difficult to dissociate emotional problems from those caused by the biological difficulties leading to mental deficiency. The mentally deficient are described as having limited ability to deal with abstract principles, language, and the use of symbols as well as having immature personalities and overly simple emotional lives. They are also described as passive but with poor impulse control and prone to repetitious behavior. To determine which characteristics arise as a direct consequence of the brain defects that cause the diminished mental abilities and those which arise from psychological reactions to their social and personal difficulties is impossible.

Finally, the problems of mentally deficient individuals are persistent. They will be with our society for many years, if not forever. To understand fully the nature of the problems of the mentally handicapped, it is necessary to understand how their brains are different from those of normal persons. The subsequent chapters will review what is known about the development of the brain, the effects of interruptions in brain development, and, most important, what these biological effects mean for the lives of the mentally deficient. Out of this knowledge it is to be hoped will come the development of an ethical policy for the mentally deficient.

Summary

The mentally deficient person is one who has severe and permanent problems in dealing with his or her environment. The charm of the *retarded child* has been lost. The hope that the child will grow out of his or her troubles has been forsaken, for the problems of the mentally deficient adult are neither minor nor transient. For the mentally deficient with moderate to profound impairment, survival would be impossible without the assistance of family or friends, acting as individuals or as agents of society. They will require help, supervision, guidance, and life-long care in order to live. The mentally handicapped need all this, and they need it in a form that is shaped by an understanding of the nature of their disorders.

TWO

Deficient Brains

While there is little doubt that normal developmental processes can be slowed or perhaps even halted by a lack of adequate stimulation, an inadequate diet, or intense emotional conflicts, most mentally defective people are that way because of disturbances in the development of the brain itself. To understand behavior, whether it be normal or abnormal, we must know about this marvelous organ and how it works. To understand the mentally deficient, we must understand why their brains work differently.

Cells of the Brain

About ten billion individual nerve cells constitute the brain. All share a special characteristic. They are like all other cells in their basic metabolic activities but, in addition, they have membranes that are capable of rapidly conducting chemical and electrical reactions. Once a membrane is excited, the disturbance rapidly spreads across all of the cell's surface. This chemical and electrical disturbance of the surface of one cell influences other cells with which it is in contact. Some of the processes of a nerve cell, usually a relatively long process called an axon, come very close to the surfaces of other cells. When the membrane disturbance reaches the end of the axon, small amounts of chemicals are released onto the surface of the adjacent cell. These chemicals begin new electrical and chemical disturbances on the membrane of the cells near the end of the axon. The chemicals released by one cell that affect the membranes of other cells are called transmitters. Not all of the cells of the brain use the same kind of transmitters. Rather, there are different types of transmitters used by different groups of cells. We do not know just how many chemicals are used as transmitters in the brain, but probably there are 20 or more different kinds. Some forms of mental deficiency, emotional disturbance, and other behavioral disorders are associated with changes in the ability of cells in the brain to produce or respond to certain transmitter substances. Nerve cell reactions and interactions are what produce mental activities and behavior. There is no other form of information processing known to occur in the brain. Thinking, acting, feelings, and emotions are all represented by the firing or nonfiring of nerve cells in the brain.

The complexities of the neuronal systems of the brain are almost beyond comprehension. Think of these ten billion nerve cells with every cell influencing thousands of others. The patterns of the firings of nerve cells going on at every moment cannot be described, but it is in these patterns of cellular activity that mental and behavioral actions are produced.

Even though we know all too little about the patterns of firing of nerve cells we do know something about the organization of the cells into groups and systems. This information comes from studies of the anatomical structure of the body and brain.

Structure of the Brain

The nerve cells that make up the brain are at the upper portion of the spinal cord. Together the brain and spinal cord make up the central nervous system. This central nervous system is surrounded by a thin layer of fluid, wrapped in the membranes and protected by bone (the skull and vertebral column). The brain and spinal cord are composed of similar materials: neurons, their processes, and supporting cells. These supporting cells are not specialized for conveying information but provide a stable and nutritive environment for nerve cells.

Many simple reflexes and movements can be executed by systems of nerve cells which exist in the spinal cord. At the top of the spinal cord where the brain begins, the neural mechanisms for some more complex behaviors are forged into the connections among nerve cells. These systems control behaviors such as walking, eating, sexual acts, elimination and can do so without requiring much help from the cells in higher regions of

26

the brain. However, these behaviors that occur without the participation of the most highly developed parts of the brain would be rather useless unless put into operation at the appropriate times and places. Therefore, even though the neural mechanisms responsible for many types of behavior exist at the upper spinal cord levels, the usefulness of the behaviors depends on selective activation by higher regions of the brain.

Three Brains

According to Dr. Paul MacLean, a noted biologist concerned with brain activities, the brain can be considered as having three major components. These are (1) the structures of the R-complex, (2) the limbic system, and (3) the neocortical surface of the brain.* The R-complex is made up of collections of nerve cells in the spinal cord and along the middle and bottom of the brain that mediate most, if not all, of the fundamental actions of animals and man (perhaps excluding language). These actions include basic behavior patterns related to fundamental biological needs and also the behaviors characteristic of animal species (e.g., stalking prey, the marking of territories, acts of aggression).

---

*Paul D. MacLean, "The Triune Brain, Emotion, and Scientific Bias." In: *The Neurosciences Second Study Program*, edited by F. O. Schmitt, New York: The Rockefeller University Press, 1970.

The neural systems responsible for these acts are thought to develop early in the life of the individual and also to be among the first to become dependent on the nervous system during the course of evolution. The mechanisms of this primitive core of all brains are capable of learning and remembering simple acts. In fact, many rather complicated forms of behavior can be executed with little more than the R-complex portions of the brains.

The second major portion of the brain, the limbic system, can be seen as a mechanism that regulates the more primitive mechanisms of the R-complex.* It adds new qualities to the lives of animals, and one way it does so is by freeing behavior from perpetual domination by the inflexible patterns of the R-complex. When the environment provides opportunities to feed, fight, drink, or engage in sexual activities, the animal must stop what it had been doing in order for the new reactions to occur. The limbic system is sensitive to the internal needs of the body and interrupts ongoing behaviors being directed by the R-complex if the new opportunity found in the environment is important to the animal. Thus, the behavior of a lion drinking

---

*See Isaacson, R. L. *The Limbic System*. New York: Plenum Press, 1974, especially chapter 6.

from a pool of water will be interrupted by the sight of prey if the lion is hungry but not if it isn't. The limbic system coordinates the conditions inside the body with environmental opportunities.

The third major structural unit to develop is that called the neomammalian brain. Probably the most important component of this part of the brain is the neocortex (neo meaning new; cortex meaning layered structure) surface. The outer rind of all mammalian brains is made up of highly specialized nerve cells arranged in layers.

The neural mechanisms of the neocortical surface of the brain represents the pinnacle of brain construction. With the appearance of the neocortex, behavioral and mental reactions become faster, perception more subtle, and most important, the future can be anticipated. In addition, language also seems to be a consequence of the development of neocortex on the left side of the brain in humans.

With mechanisms for foresight and planning, animals are further freed from the domination by habitual ways of responding. Plans can be made for tomorrow, next week, next year, and even for future generations. To do so, however, requires that the habitual or instinctive ways of responding become suppressed when they are no longer useful.

The formation of the brain of every individual begins with development of the R-complex, and is followed by the limbic system and the neocortex. In humans all of the nerve cells of all three systems are formed before birth. However, while all of the nerve cells are formed, not all systems are operational at that time. Many pathways connecting cells in one part of the brain with cells in other parts are incomplete. So are the mechanisms responsible for the manufacture of certain of the chemical messengers. Some parts of the brain will not be fully functional until puberty.

At birth many mechanisms of the R-complex are ready for action, but only a few of those in the limbic or neocortical systems are. The baby is ready to breathe, suck, eliminate, regulate body temperature, cry, and exhibit gross body movements. All of these are regulated by neural systems within the R-complex. It will be over the next months and years that systems of limbic and neocortical groups become functional.

The master plan responsible for the formation of body and brain dictates that particular groups of cells will be formed but according to a strict time schedule. Because of the special significance of this master building plan for mental deficiency, we must consider it in greater detail.

The Formation of the Brain and Body

Life begins at the penetration of the egg by a sperm. This one single fertilized cell contains all of the instructions required for the formation of the individual. These instructions received from the genes supplied by both the father and the mother represent a unique combination of genetic instructions. These instructions provide for an uncountable number of organs, processes, and systems in the body and brain.

The finished body is made up of millions upon millions of cells and their products. A metaphor that may help in the understanding of the development of the body is to consider the individual cells of the body as "people" living in close contact with each other in a large modern city.

Consider for a moment the instructions that would be necessary to organize a city of a billion or so people from the very start. All of the various services required by the population would have to be planned, jobs assigned, materials provided, people placed in appropriate locations, communication among groups of people arranged, and methods established for the removal of waste products.

Biologically, the master plan as well as plans for special subsystems are incorporated into the person's genetic inheritance. Included in these plans must be one for growth.

How can the city grow from its very first inhabitant (the fertilized egg) to its full complement of individuals in a very short period of time?

The instructions for the building of the individual are sometimes called genetic information. As can be imagined, the information required to build a body with all of its many functions must be enormous.

Genetic information is written into the cells of the body as an incredibly large number of coded instructions, like dots and dashes, which are contained in long molecules (DNA) tucked into the nucleus of each and every cell. These long DNA molecules break apart when the egg and sperm are formed. One-half of the DNA usually found in a complete cell goes into each sperm or egg. When the egg and the sperm unite to form the new person, the two half-amounts combine to provide the full DNA complement again. However, the DNA is in a new form that differs from what it was in either parent, and the new person has a unique combination of traits, structures, and processes, different from any person who has ever lived before. But the new person does, of course, share some characteristics of his or her ancestors from whom DNA has been contributed over many generations.

The genetic information specifies the precise birthdays for each type of cell. Cells destined to be specific portions of the R-complex, the limbic system, or the neocortex are formed on specific days and on no others. Indeed, it is possible that some classes of nerve cells are formed only within a period of a few hours. After that period has passed, no other cells like them will be formed.

Nerve cells are only formed at particular times and when they die or are destroyed by accident, they are gone forever. Since the cellular structures of the brain are made in accordance with a rigid, inexorable time-table, the analogy would say that squads of people in our mythic city of the body arrived on a predetermined schedule: Monday, builders and construction workers; Tuesday, food handlers; Wednesday, sanitary engineers; Thursday, electricians; Friday, road-builders, and so on. The last groups of workers to be formed would be those with the neocortical jobs: librarians, news-fore-casters, judges, and pundits.

One important implication of this rigid time schedule is that if an interruption in the formation of nerve cells occurs at some point there is no catching up. Cells still capable of cell division do not go back to make up losses incurred by the interruption. This, in turn, means that the successful completion of any brain region depends on the formation of the appropriate number of cells *at a particular time*. Moreover, the formation of a particular brain system also depends on the prior formation of other structures and cells. Therefore, disturbances of the baby's developing brain, even if they last only a brief period of time, can have extensive effects, not only on the cells and systems being formed at that time but also on all the cells and systems formed afterwards.

Genetic Deficiencies

Returning to the analogy of our city of a billion people, what would happen if some of the instructions for building the city were lost or changed? If the instructions pertaining to a city's vital activities were wrong, life would not be possible. If there were inadequate ways to obtain food or to eliminate wastes, the city would fail. Other plans are less essential to the life of the city. For example, if plans for libraries were not quite right the city might still survive. Abnormalities of development can affect any of the body's organs. If organs related to the vital functions of the individual are affected, life is not possible. This means that if the genetic instructions for creation of the heart, lungs, kidney, liver and other vital organs are not appropriate, the baby will not survive. On the other hand, erroneous plans for some aspects of the body are less harmful to life. People can live with malformed bones and muscles, short limbs, poorly formed eyes and ears.

Some mentally deficient people have received incorrect genetic plans. This can occur in several ways. It can be the consequence of receiving poor "instructions" from one or both parents. The parents may not have been affected because information about the building of the body and brain exists in duplicate in the hereditary materials. Each person has two doses of information and one dose is usually dominant and the other recessive. The instructions for the poor formation of the body or the brain may be recessive in both parents but hidden in them by the dominant instructions. However, if two recessive doses, both containing abnormal building plans, are received by the baby, abnormal development could occur despite apparently normal parents.

The genetic information may be inappropriate for still other reasons. In the case of Mongolism, the affected person has received too much information in the form of an extra chromosome. Often it is impossible to tell why this has happened. (It should be noted that some people can be carriers of Mongolism. The parents of all Mongoloid children should seek genetic counseling.) In certain instances a child will receive inappropriate genetic instructions despite a normal genetic make-up of both parents. The cause of these spontaneous disruptions of the genetic instructions are largely unknown.

We do not know exactly why genetic inadequacies lead to mental deficiency. Sometimes the genetic instructions for supplying nutritional materials to the cells are wrong, sometimes too much or too little of a certain chemical transmitter is made, and other times too few cells are created. In still other conditions the actual structure of the body and brain are incorrect. The end result, however, is a collection of systems that do not work correctly and mental deficiency results.

Disturbances of Development

Accidents sometimes happen to the mother or to the developing baby that interrupt the formation of nerve cells during the development. These can be due to inappropriate genetic instructions or to disease, drugs, or trauma to mother and child, or for other often unknown reasons.

Mental deficiency could result from disturbances affecting the three major types of brain structures: the R-complex; the limbic system; or the neomammalian systems. Accidents occurring earliest in the fetal period would produce disruptions of the R-complex, accidents occurring somewhat later would affect the limbic system, and accidents occurring near the end of gestation would selectively influence the neomammalian systems.

Severe disruptions of the R-complex produce such major problems that life itself is usually forfeit. If individuals with damage to the R-complex survive, they would exhibit mental and physical deficiencies of the most profound character. Furthermore, since any anomaly of brain development affects all later developing systems, disturbances of formation of the R-complex will also lead to abnormal development in the limbic and neomammalian systems.

Accidents that occur to the developing baby at later times can affect the formation of the limbic and neomammalian systems. However, disruptions at the time of formation of the R-complex and limbic system will also induce alterations in the neomammalian system because without proper formation of the first two systems, the neural basis for the development of neomammalian brain is lacking. This means that developmental disturbances at any time before birth will result in aberrant development of the neocortical systems. Because of the universal involvement of the neomammalian brain systems in instances of brain damage, it is necessary to consider the nature of the mental and behavioral deficits that result from damage to the neocortex.

Damage restricted to portions of the neocortical surface often does *not* produce catastrophic distortions of behavior, although there are measurable disturbances in both motor and sensory capabilities. Rather, it is the fine movements and subtle perceptions that become lost after neocortical damage. The more fundamental abilities to move, get along in the world, learn and remember are not destroyed. It is only those movements, thoughts, and actions that go well beyond the commonplace, the extraordinary accomplishments, for which the neocortex is essential. Projections of future events would be a case in point. People with damage restricted to the most frontal portions of the brain's surface, for example, tend to be uninterested in the potential joys or dangers of the future. They tend to live for the moment. They are not ill-suited for basic biological survival, but they miss many of the pleasures which come from anticipation of the future.

Accidental damage to the neocortex of the adult seldom results in behavior that is like that of the mentally deficient. A person with neocortical damage may have obvious speech problems, perceptual distortions, or slowed reactions, but not those global problems associated with mental deficiency.

Most frequently, damage to the limbic system in the human adult is the consequence of metabolic disturbances, stroke, or tumors. Often such damage leads to the production of an epileptic condition in the area of damage. If this happens, the patient's behavior not only reflects the absence of certain neural systems but the epileptic disorder as well. People with limbic system disorders often are prone to fits of anger and aggression, sometimes with a sexual theme. They may have disturbed eating and drinking patterns and consequently have weight regulation problems. They also have trouble in suppression of older memories and this seems to interfere with recalling recent events. Yet, in talking with these patients, an observer does not get the impression of mental deficiency. They seem to have a memory disorder or other behavioral problems, but they are not mistaken for mentally deficient people.

As mentioned before, people with damage to the R-complex in adulthood are unlikely to resemble the mentally deficient because they are not likely to live. The mechanisms which are served by the R-complex are so vital to survival that life is impossible if they are damaged.

Hence, although all cases of restricted brain damage in adulthood cause specific behavior alterations, these rarely resemble the behavioral characteristics of the mentally deficient. The only brain damaged adults who resemble those with mental deficiencies are those with widespread, diffuse damage, and such widespread damage is quite rare. Only brain damage occurring before birth or early in life is likely to lead to the widespread damage that causes a broad range of mental and physical difficulties.

Anatomical Changes Associated with Mental Deficiency

Events that cause the death of cells or the temporary suppression of cell division can lead to many different kinds of brain abnormalities depending on when they occur. One certain consequence, however, would be the reduction in the number of nerve cells in the brain. This is related in turn to the consistent observation that the brains (and heads) of many mentally deficient people are smaller than their nonretarded contemporaries. The actual number of cells destroyed is difficult to determine because there are so many cells involved, ten billion or so. A loss of several millions of cells would be undetectable. Moreover, the supportive cells, the glia, sometimes resemble small neurons and special techniques must be used to distinguish them from nerve cells.

Despite these problems in determining just what has happened, it appears that most mental deficiency is associated with a reduction in the number of nerve cells and an increase in the number of supportive glia cells which cannot substitute for nerve cells.

Other changes in the brain associated with mental deficiency can be even more subtle and hence harder to detect. They include changes at the points of contact between nerve cells. These changes would make the interaction among nerve cells less efficient.

Further, the changes which occur because of accidents in development can lead to alterations in the chemistry of the brain rather than to structural malformations. If the specifications of but a single enzyme are altered, the formation of one or more types of transmitter substance is not possible. The brain has fewer chemical messengers. This can lead to extensive behavioral disabilities.

When any part of the brain fails to be formed correctly, subsequent anatomical regions will also develop incorrectly. Sometimes the major structures of the brain appear to be normal, but the connections among them are not.

Other factors tend to obscure the precise nature of the disarrangement of the anatomical problems associated with mental deficiencies so that it has not been possible to pinpoint the time at which the development of the brain goes wrong. As more and more is learned about the development of the brain and how interruptions of brain development are reflected in permanent antomical changes, it will be possible to know just when things have gone wrong. This information could help in developing new treatments that would allow the brain to restore lost cells, reduce the development of aberrant structures formed at later times, and consequently reduce the loss in mental capacities. Prenatal intervention with the developing fetus to minimize the effects of an accident occurring before birth is one of the ways in which mental deficiency will become less frequent. This goal may not be too far distant: 50 to 100 years, perhaps. Until then, the mentally deficient will be with us.

Summary

This chapter has provided an overview of some of the basic biological mechanisms underlying the function of the brain and how mental deficiency results from widespread alterations in the function of the brain. These changes are most likely to occur because of faulty genetic instructions or some accident affecting the development of the brain. Brain damage in adulthood may produce specific alterations in mental activities or behavior but not the more global problems seen in the mentally deficient. Damage that affects the developing brain early in prenatal life will also influence the development of all subsequently formed regions. For this reason, the effects of damage at any prenatal period will affect a variety of structures and systems.

Despite years of research, we know all too little about the behavioral contribution of different regions of the brain. But certain rather general statements can be made about the basic behavioral mechanisms of the R-complex and about the special contributions made by the structures of the limbic and neomammalian systems. The analysis of these behavioral correlates of brain activity will be continued in the next chapter.

THREE

Mental and Behavioral Problems of the Mentally Deficient

Perhaps at some future time specific behavioral changes will be linked to specific alterations in the brain structure or function. Unfortunately, this cannot be achieved at present, for we know too little about the relationship of particular brain regions to behavior. We do know, however, a reasonable amount about the behavior of the mentally deficient. Coupling this information with informed guesses derived from knowledge of the brain can lead us toward a better understanding of some of the problems of the mentally deficient.

Disorders of Movement

One of the most common characteristics of brain damage that occurs at almost any time before birth is a disturbance of motor movements. This can be reflected in a general awkwardness, clumsy walk, weakness, and an inability to achieve fine control of the fingers. Sometimes there is a progressive increase in the tendency to contract the large muscles that move the limbs toward the body. This is one of the symptoms of cerebral palsy.

Because very young children have such limited behavioral capacities, many motor disturbances are difficult to detect in the first few months of life. Yet if there is a severe amount of brain damage before birth, some motor disturbances will be seen at birth or shortly afterwards. Sometimes this is observed during nursing, as seen in difficulties in finding and keeping the nipple, or just by low muscle tone. Mothers often are aware of potential mental deficiencies in their children through the peculiar ways in which their babies feel or nurse.

Mongoloid children have a pronounced reduction in muscle tone because of an abnormally low amount of a specific transmitter substance in their bodies and brain. Muscle tonicity can be restored by the administration of medicines which increase this particular substance. However, the restoration of muscle tonicity does not improve mental abilities. Therefore, while abnormal motor abilities and mental retardation are found together in Mongoloid children, they are independent consequences of aberrant brain development.

The motor disturbances associated with mental deficiency are the reason why there must be "Special Olympics." If the mentally deficient had only mental problems they could compete in the regular Olympics. Their motor disturbances are responsible, in part, for the difficulties encountered by the mentally deficient in doing delicate work, playing musical instruments, and being successful in other tasks where fine coordinated, or delicate movements are required.

Incoordination and poor muscular control can also be responsible for the poor writing abilities often seen in the mildly mentally deficient. This suggests that ways should be found to minimize the handicap by the use of easy-to-operate electric typewriters and other appropriately designed mechanical devices. The need to correct visual or hearing defects in all children is well accepted, but motor disturbances present special problems for which there can be some compensation through special training as well as through physical aids.

Motor Coordination and Esteem

Athletic ability is used by both peers and family as a measure of a person's value. The boy who is first chosen for athletic teams, who demonstrates ability and desire in competitive sports, is highly valued. The awkward, gangly boy, chosen last or ignored by others when the teams are picked, is not. Both types of boy come to share the opinions held by his family and friends. Athletic ability as a basis of evaluation is not restricted to children. The good golfer is thought to be a better person than the duffer who seldom breaks a hundred. The awkwardness of the mentally deficient person was a handicap from the very beginning relative to the more highly developed abilities of nonretarded associates. Today, athletic abilities and more coordination are important for both girls and boys. In the past girls were esteemed for their graceful movements, dexterity, dancing, and other activities for which elegant control of their bodies is required, but there is an ever increasing tendency to value and prize motor skills regardless of the sex of the participant.

Mentally deficient persons begin life with motor handicaps that make them less desirable group members. The individual is placed near the bottom of the social hierarchy because of this nonintellectual problem. The result of low peer group value is low self-esteem. Even for a nondeficient person it would be hard to achieve greater self-confidence and assurance.

Activity

A frequently discussed problem is that of hyperactivity in children. Children called hyperactive often have problems in school, stemming from an inability to keep their attention on assignments, difficulty in controlling their impulses, and an inability to remain quietly in their seats. They often have a disruptive influence on the rest of the class. As the hyperactive child grows older, he may become less active physically, but this does not mean his schoolwork will improve. Sometimes the inability to maintain attention on one task and keep impulses under control remains throughout life.

A biological basis for some forms of hyperactivity is indicated by the fact that amphetamine and related drugs can improve the performance of the hyperactive child, including difficulties of motor movements, attention, and impulse control. This is a paradoxical effect of the drugs, since in normal children, the drugs will produce hyperactivity rather than decrease it. However, not all hyperactive children respond favorably to these drugs. This suggests that there are different forms of hyperactivity and only some are remedied by drugs.

Several years ago I had an opportunity to visit an experimental program for about fifteen hyperactive children. All of the children had been asked to withdraw from regular or special classes in the public schools. In this program all were under amphetamine or amphetaminelike drugs and most were able to work well under the close supervision provided in the special program. However, even with the medication and the close, one-to-one attention being provided, the children were easily disrupted from their work by any unusual occurrence in the room and some had increasing bouts of distraction as the morning progressed. One boy apologized to his teacher for beginning to be a "bad boy" but said he just couldn't help himself. By carefully comparing the effects obtained with times of medication, the staff were able to show that the beginning of poor behavioral control was related to the wearing off of the drug rather than events in the class or fatigue.

Hypoactive (less active than normal) children and adults have been studied less because they present fewer problems to teachers and parents. The hypoactive child often is thought to be well-behaved. Parents may state that they wish their other children were as good. However, the excessively quiet child may not be exploring his world, testing his ideas, or trying new things. In the long run, the hypoactive child may not be any better off than the hyperactive child.

Studies of disruption in brain formation before birth in experimental animals indicate that either hypoactivity or hyperactivity may result, depending on when the interruption occurred.

Physical Appearance

Many people share a myth that mentally deficient children are attractive, cute, and lovable. This is not the case. Anyone who has visited institutions for the mentally deficient or even special education classes, realizes the opposite is more often true. For the most part, the mentally deficient are less attractive than their nondeficient contemporaries. Faces, physique, hair, eyes, and other physical attributes are often unpleasant. Many people find it difficult even to be around the mentally handicapped because of their outward appearance.

While some mentally deficient people have misshapen bodies and heads as a consequence of arrest of brain development that led to the deficiency, there may be deformations of other organs, too. Heart, kidneys, and endocrine gland defects all can occur as a consequence of the difficulty that led to the brain defect. Any of the individual's facial and physical characteristics can be altered by aberrations of development. These include small or misplaced eyes, malformations of the palate, peculiar formation of the ears, and major skeletal deformations.

A lessened physical attractiveness tends to produce low self-esteem, since physical attractiveness is a valued characteristic in our culture. Beauty opens many doors and leads to many opportunities. Therefore, just as with motor coordination, the mentally deficient person is frequently at a handicap throughout life because of factors other than mental. For example, only in the most advanced institutions are beauty parlours and barber shops available for residents. Seldom are programs or facilities designed to make the mentally deficient person more attractive. To the extent that the mentally deficient can be trained to improve their appearance, social acceptance and self-esteem would be improved.

The Emotions

Another common myth is that most mentally deficient people are always happy. Those who think of mentally deficient adults as large-bodied children also think them to have childish emotions. In reality, many mentally deficient people are dissatisfied with their lot in life, saddened by the reactions of others to them, and frustrated by a lack of opportunity to do what they see others doing. Mildly and moderately mentally deficient people experience the most anxiety and unhappiness from these causes, but probably all mentally deficient people can sense rejection. There is, however, also no doubt that many mentally deficient individuals do react quite differently to situations and people. Some are slow to anger and show exaggerated affection toward almost everyone. Some of the mentally deficient are sullen and withdrawn. Some are hostile (but the actively aggressive person is rare). Both fear and

53

affection are easily learned by mentally deficient people and, once learned, tend to persist.

Some of the fears of the mentally deficient are specific to situations that do not usually produce fear in nondeficient people. For example, some can be terrified of being on slight elevations, such as on a ledge a foot or two high, while unafraid of the deep end of a swimming pool even though they cannot swim and have had to be rescued after falling in before. The unusual fear of heights often found in the mentally deficient was exemplified recently in what I saw in a private day care facility. A boy about 11 years of age was being encouraged to go through a simple obstacle course to help him improve his motor abilities. He was able to go through all of the course with relative ease until he came to a small bridge. The height was about eight inches above the ground with gentle ramps at both ends. A hand rail was provided. Everytime he came to this short bridge he stopped and looked about in terror. Two aides had to help him over, each holding one of his hands. He had evidenced the same type of behavior for a month. The fear of even minor heights found in some of the mentally handicapped may explain their reluctance to go up or down stairs, a characteristic often observed.

Probably both the abnormal fear reactions and a general tendency toward placidity are consequences of abnormalities in the limbic system.

Epilepsy

A large percentage of all mentally deficient people suffer from some form of seizure disorder. All forms of seizures are referred to as epilepsy even though the actual behavioral changes can be quite different. All are thought to be due to abnormal electrical activities produced near a site of damage that spread widely throughout the brain. The reason why so many mentally deficient people also suffer from epilepsy is unknown.

A form of epilepsy called temporal lobe epilepsy is *sometimes* associated with sudden and unprovocated outbursts of rage. Most people with temporal lobe epilepsy do not have these outbursts. Only a very, very few people with this type of epilepsy do. But, if the disease does express itself in this way, the person may strike out at whomever is nearby when the attack occurs. The person with the convulsion takes up any object within reach to use as a weapon. The attacks are well directed; those unfortunate enough to be close by when they occur are often hurt and sometimes killed.

Several years ago I met a young black woman about sixteen years old who was in a state institution for the mentally deficient. She was reasonably attractive and only mildly deficient and would have been a likely person for supervised living in the community except for her violent outbursts. Two or three times a week, at completely unpredictable times and places, she would strike out at anyone or anything around. The episodes lasted from about five to fifteen minutes after which she returned to being a normal quiet woman. Being physically strong, she was able to do a great deal of damage, often destroying all of the furniture and fixtures in the room where she was when the episode occurred. One time it happened in a multiple bedroom. All of the beds were destroyed to the level of wood kindling and mattress fluff. Fortunately, a temporal lobe epilepsy was diagnosed and she proved responsive to anticonvulsant medication before she seriously injured anyone. No seizures have occurred while she is on the medication but often she fails to take the medication. Constant surveillance is necessary to insure that she does.

Temporal lobe epilepsy can also express itself in other ways. These include moments in which the person seems to be out of touch with reality. At other times the person will say

56

or do bizarre things which are not remembered later. Neurologically, temporal lobe epilepsy originates in the temporal lobe of the brain and spreads to limbic system structures in the same region.

Learning, Memory, and Performance

To understand the effects of aberrant brain development on learning, memory, and performance, it is first necessary to eliminate a few common, but incorrect, assumptions. The first is that learning and memory represent the summit, the pinnacle, of human brain development. The fact is that the ability to learn and to remember is common to all forms of animal life, even those made up of only a few cells. Species that some people think of as lower forms of animal life, such as rats, cats, dogs, fish, all have remarkable capacities for learning and memory. For the learning of some things, these lower animals may do better than people.

A second misconception is that learning and memory are dependent on the most highly developed portions of brain (the neocortical areas). In fact, many forms of learning can take place with almost all of the neocortex destroyed. There have even been studies in which rapid learning occurs in animals with little more than the R-complex remaining.

A third misconception is that all learning and memory are alike. In fact there are many forms of learning and many forms of memory. We learn verbal responses quite differently from the way we learn to hit a golf ball. The retention of these different types of learning is quite different, too. Memories are stored in many different ways. There are visual memories, motor memories, short-term memories, and long-term memories. There are emotional memories and memories for facts. All involve different neural systems of the brain.

A fourth misconception is that the mentally deficient are deficient in learning and/or memory. The fact is that many of the mentally deficient can learn simple problems faster than nonretarded people and retain them longer.

Repudiation of this last misconception is important, since it is a mistake to think of mentally deficient people as suffering from a learning impairment. The mentally handicapped may have learning difficulties in some areas, but a general loss in either learning or memory abilities is not their problem. Furthermore, since learning and memory are often independent of each other, people may have independent changes in each faculty.

58

The widespread combination of overly rapid learning of simple things and extraordinarily strong rentention often works to the disadvantage of the mentally deficient. The extraordinary retention of previously learned materials can easily be seen as a behavioral handicap. The dogged preservation of an inappropriate behavior clearly is not useful, while rapid forgetting of what has been learned and even the ability to learn new responses quickly can also be troublesome. The more rapidly an individual learns a response, the more susceptible behavior is to transitory changes of the environment. The most adaptive behavior represents a balance between a reluctance to change behavior on the basis of every slight change in the environment and a dogged preservation of previously learned responses that are clearly no longer useful. A beneficial approach to events in the environment requires gradually modified behaviors and not ones that are either constantly or never changing.

Recently I watched a sixteen-year-old Mongoloid girl learning to assemble 35mm photographic film canisters in a rehabilitation center. She had been trained previously with a slightly different type of film canister but needed to be entirely retrained in the procedure despite the fact that the new canister was different in only one small way from the former model. She ritualistically persisted in the previously learned steps. The only way the professionals had found effective in changing her behavior was to start the whole training process over with a somewhat different organization of materials. For this girl, the previously learned procedures, once started, just had to be carried to completion, regardless of their appropriateness.

The Neurology of Performance

While damage to any particular part of the brain does not seem to influence the memory of previously learned responses, damage to certain regions of the brain can influence a person's actions. For example, damage to one portion of the limbic system makes it difficult for animals to begin new responses, while damage to another portion of the limbic system allows animals to undertake new responses more readily than intact animals. This is of significance for training the mentally deficient to do new things, since the more readily responses are undertaken, the sooner they can be learned.

I remember observing a young Mongoloid girl watch several nondeficient children of about her age go in and out of a door. She clearly wanted to open the door like the other children but was reluctant to try, probably because the door had an unfamiliar handle. She kept watching the handle after the other children had all left the room. Slowly and tentatively she left her chair, went over and touched the handle. Nothing happened. She went back and sat down, still keeping her attention fixed on it. It took about ten trips before she managed to get a firm grip on the handle and open the door. Certainly, this extensive probing of the new handle may be related to a fear of unknown stimuli, but the problem was the extended period during which no responses were made. Once a full response was made and the door opened, she never had trouble with it again. Her learning abilities were not changed in this situation, only the tendency to make the first new response. This sort of change should be called a performance change to distinguish it from the abilities to learn or remember.

From experimental studies of animals it appears that damage to the limbic system results in several types of performance changes: changes in ability to initiate new responses, impaired retrieval of stored memories, difficulties in giving up previously learned reactions, overreactions to changes in the environment, and an insensitivity to changes in rewards.

Many mentally deficient persons have behavioral problems of this nature. Many have trouble giving up previously learned reactions. For example, if a mentally deficient boy is taught to say eight when asked how old he is, often it is hard to teach him to say nine in response to the same question a year later. However, some mentally deficient people are too quick to start new things. Many, also, are very upset and afraid when the environment is not what it usually is. New schedules, room arrangements, food, lighting, or what-have-you often result in intense emotional reactions. When something is displaced in their world, they cannot seem to rest until the usual order is restored.

Since many characteristics of limbic system damage seem to be found in the behavior of the mentally deficient, it could be hypothesized that the disturbances of brain development leading to their condition may have occurred at the time the limbic system was being formed. And, since the formation of one system depends on the prior formation of earlier systems, interference with the formation of the limbic system is likely to result in aberrant formation of *both* the limbic and neocortical systems. As damage occurs later in gestation, closer to the time of birth, the defect will be more and more restricted to the neocortical systems.

Behavioral Effects of Neocortical Damage

Despite the fact that there has been more research undertaken on the functional characteristics of the neocortical surface of the brain than on the functions of any other brain region, less is known about how this tissue contributes to behavior than about other brain regions.

Destruction of the neocortical surface produces many different types of changes. The type of change depends on the area of the neocortical surface which is destroyed. For example, damage to the middle area of the neocortical surface reduces motor coordination speed in movement. Damage to the posterior regions of the brain surface reduces the ability to make fine visual discriminations. Often these changes in the sensory abilities of the individual are slight and difficult to detect. Damage to the temporal lobes along the sides of the brain, just in from the ears, reduces the ability to recognize sound patterns, although there is no alteration in the ability to detect the presence, frequency, or intensity of sounds. On the top of the left temporal lobe there are areas that are almost exclusively involved in the utilization of language. There are several language-related areas of the neocortex on the left side of the brain. Some are involved with understanding speech, some with the production of speech, and still others with reading and writing, i.e., written speech.

In recent years other important distinctions between the right and left sides of the brain have been recognized. While the left seems to be especially suited for the development of linguistic abilities, the right tends to have special capabilities for the analysis of spatial relationships. These differences in the functions of the right and left sides of the human brain are found in the vast majority of adults, whether they are right- or left-handed. However, the specialization of the two sides is not an inevitable consequence of development. If damage occurs to the left early in life, adequate language capabilities can develop—presumably localized on the right side. Similarly, if damage occurs to the right side early in life, the left seems to have the ability to become responsible for the organization of the spatial world.

Hence developmental pecularities that result in inappropriate formation of the neocortical surface of the brain may lead to a variety of behavioral problems. These include visual and auditory distortions, a spatial disorganization of the environment, and difficulties with speech and language that can manifest themselves in several ways.

The most anterior portions of the neocortex are important for making plans for the future. Emotional changes also occur with damage to these anterior regions. The most common consequence of such damage is that both the positive and negative consequences seem to lose importance for the person involved. It is as if the emotions had been severely blunted.

In the structure of the neocortex, the arrangement of cells and their functions is one of great elegance and complexity. It should not be surprising that damage to the neocortical surface produces subtle, hard-to-describe changes in behavior. It is the author's opinion that this happens because the neocortical mantle is not a basic mechanism responsible for behavioral processes such as perception, learning, memory, or motor behavior. Rather, it is a specialized type of tissue that prepares the organism for future actions. To do so, it must evaluate the present state of the organism, consider the present conditions of the environment, and then proceed to make calculations about the rewards to be derived from possible future actions. Hence its main focus of interest is the future rather than the present.

To take advantage of the environmental opportunities, the neocortex must suppress behaviors that are no longer rewarded. This is done by the neocortex influencing certain portions of the limbic system which in turn suppresses activities being governed by the R-complex. In this manner the neocortex and the limbic system act together to regulate the oldest, most conservative, portions of the brain so that new forms of behavior can occur.

Many years ago, Sigmund Freud postulated that human behavior operates in accord with one of two basic principles. One of these was the *pleasure principle* in which the immediate satisfaction of needs and desires was sought. He thought the infant whose hunger immediately initiated actions directed toward taking in the nipple was demonstrating behavior based on the pleasure principle. As a need or desire occurs, immediate satisfaction is demanded. With advancing age, children and adults come to be able to postpone gratification of their needs in light of environmental circumstances. Food incorporation and elimination are postponed until circumstances are appropriate. Sexual behavior is not demonstrated when the desire is felt, but postponed until the conditions are reasonably appropriate. This postponement of desires reflects behavior based on the *reality principle*. In other words, when people act in accordance with the *reality principle* they delay gratification of their needs because of a greater reward associated with the delay. This delay of gratification depends on the anticipation of future benefits to be derived from waiting which in turn depends on appropriate activities of the neocortex.

The mentally deficient person often finds it hard to delay the gratification of desires and demands. This could be due to a decreased ability to inhibit actions (limbic system damage) or to a difficulty in anticipating the future values and costs of specific behaviors (neocortical damage) or both. It might be thought that as a result, mentally defective people would engage in sexual or aggressive acts. However, for a number of reasons, including a fear of the unusual and of social disapproval, and possibly a lessened interest in sexual matters, this is not usually the case. Further, even though they may not understand the immediate and future consequences of their actions, most mentally deficient persons can be trained to exhibit appropriate styles of behavior. By such training, behavior can be made socially appropriate even though the reasons behind the behavior may not be understood.

Another aspect of behavioral deficiency arising from neocortical damage is a loss in imagination. Most nondeficient adults have rich fantasy lives. This is not an insignificant loss, since fantasy can be used to explore possible actions without their actual execution. In fantasy a person can imagine numerous possible actions and make estimates of their consequences. A deficiency in the development of the neocortical surface would weaken the development of fantasy and imagination in general.

Many of the day-to-day actions required in modern society have to do with the anticipation of the future. These problems range from the buying of insurance and planning of budgets to religion and many other aspects of life. Without the ability to comprehend the importance of health care, insurance, and budget planning, life becomes more stressful and dangerous. The handicap in planning ahead is important, not only for the lives of the mentally deficient themselves, but for all those with whom they are associated.

Summary

One of the most common characteristics of mentally deficient people is a disturbance in simple motor abilities. They are generally awkward and unable to execute delicate motor acts. They also may have changes in activity levels and emotional reactions. These characteristics, coupled with a tendency to be less attractive physically, put the deficient disadvantage in competition with the nondeficient even aside from their mental problems.

Abnormal brain development results in permanent abnormalties in structure and function of both the limbic and neomammalian (neocortical) portions of the brain. The limbic system changes are reflected in changes of performances but *not* in alterations of learning or memory abilities. Also common is the loss of a capacity to base present actions on predictions of what will happen in the future. This capacity is dependent on the proper formation of the neomammalian brain.

FOUR

The Mentally Deficient Person in Society

In the previous chapters the biological basis for mental deficiency and some of the behavioral effects of these changes have been described. The behavior of mentally deficient people *is* different from that of non-deficient people. They are *different*. As a consequence, they are "special people," out-of-step with the rest of the world, separated and estranged.

Views of the Mentally Deficient Person

A Child

For some people, mentally deficient persons of any age are children. It is assumed that they started life just as everyone else, but that something happened along the way to freeze their development prior to adulthood. This view is bolstered by the fact that mentally deficient children often seem to follow a normal course of development for the first few months of life. Abnormalities only become apparent as the child grows older. This notion of an arrested development in the mentally deficient person is reflected in the use of the term *retarded*.

Following this approach, mentally deficient people are thought to have a permanent childlike disposition. Many people, professionals included, refer to the mentally deficient as children, even though the "child" may be fifty or sixty years old. This view fosters a paternalistic and overprotective attitude toward the deficient. It also allows the unrealistic hope that whatever has blocked normal development may be removed in some magical way.

By now it should be clear that the mentally deficient person is not a child who never grew up. The deficiencies in the structure and function of the brain have led to differences in behavioral capacities that will be more, not less, apparent as the person grows older. Early in life these differences are hidden because most of the baby's actions are governed by the neural systems formed before the damage occurred to the developing brain. The apparently normal behavior seen just after birth is only an indication of the operation of a relatively intact R-complex portion of the brain. These systems are responsible for such fundamental acts as eating, drinking, sleeping, and elimination. If their formation had been interrupted, the fetus would not have survived. As the child develops after birth, behavior becomes more and more dependent on the later developing limbic and neocortical systems. As a result, more and more behavioral abnormalities are seen as the child matures.

A Person From a Different Culture

Sometimes a mentally deficient person is thought of as basically like us but as coming from a different culture. This implies that the mentally deficient person is someone with different customs, habits, values, ways of measuring time and money, needs and expressions. Little thought is given as to why these different characteristics came about. No thought is given to the fact that most mentally deficient people develop in our culture, in "normal" homes with "normal" mothers, fathers, sisters, and brothers. As a metaphor used to understand them, the different culture interpretation is valueless. Nevertheless, we hear people compare the mentally deficient with the Eskimo or the Bantu or people from other remote places. The fact that the Eskimo tells time by "sleeps" and "moons" instead of hours, minutes, or seconds does not make him like the mentally deficient person who cannot learn to tell time by any means. In the Eskimo's view, the watch reveals unimportant information which he sees no reason to learn even though he could, but many mentally deficient cannot learn this skill even though it might be helpful to them.

Some extremists of the culturally different interpretation of mental deficiency have suggested that mentally handicapped people

74

be allowed to establish their own cultures. Left to their own devices, the mentally deficient would not establish a culture. Within a brief period of time a group of mentally deficient individuals would perish even in circumstances of abundance.

The culturally different approach is as much nonsense as that which pictures the mentally deficient as an arrested child. The mentally deficient person has trouble in all cultures. There are no simple cultures. All are complex in customs, policies, history, and the patterns of behavior expected from their members. Dull-witted individuals have problems in all societies. In the Eskimo culture of the Deer People, the mentally deficient person only survives because of the generosity of his friends and neighbors. In our culture mentally deficient people also survive by the good works of a friend or neighbor, except in those few areas in which adequate social services are available to fill their needs.

A Special Infirmity

Another view of mentally deficient people is that they are like us except for special infirmities primarily in the educational realm. According to this view, their problem is dealing with the abstractions required to read and make numerical calculations. These abilities are prerequisites for education and, to this extent, a loss of the ability to use abstract concepts is a handicap. However, this position is often pushed further by saying that while the mentally deficient suffer from an educational handicap, this is their only failing. It is extended even further by the argument that since their handicap is only in the realm of complicated matters of education and related matters of modern technology, the mentally deficient could have survived and perhaps even gone unnoticed under simpler conditions of life.

This approach is misleading in two regards. First, it assumes that the mentally deficient are only limited in matters related to the abilities required for success in the modern educational system. This is not true even for those only mildly deficient. Second, like the other culture theory, it assumes that earlier cultures were simpler than our own.

Neither Western nor Eastern societies were that much simpler several hundred years ago or even a couple of thousand years ago. Many of the same sorts of problems existed then as do now. Survival was, in fact, more difficult, because the penalties of famine, disease, and political change were harsher then than now. In many areas all of a person's cunning and skills were required just to stay alive. Improving a person's quality of life required extraordinary skill since employment opportunities were limited by a person's family history and social class. The expression of mental abilities varied from rural to city life, but success required a high level of mental capacities in both circumstances. As a consequence, the mentally impaired person has been handicapped throughout history.

As has been seen, the mentally deficient have a wide range of behavioral and thinking difficulties, some related to educational success, but many related to other problems of day-to-day life.

The simplistic behavioral psychology so prevalent in the United States during the 1940s and 1950s has contributed much to this misconception of the mentally deficient as persons with just an educational handicap. In most theories of that era, behavior was thought to depend only on the appropriate connection of stimuli with responses.

According to this view, the person is a blank slate, written on by experience in the form of associations between stimuli and responses. One of the early spokesmen for the behavioristic movement used to state that given control of a child early enough, it could be made into any type of person, doctor, lawyer, or Indian chief. The contribution of heredity was minimized, if not denied entirely. Relative to mental deficiency, one might ask, "Can one slate be blanker than another?"

The ideas of these early behaviorists permeated the fields of education and the social sciences. All behavior was held to be the result of the environment. The delinquent, the insane, the mentally deficient were all products of unfortunate environments.

If one grants the assumption that unfortunate behavior is the consequence of unfortunate prior learning, the defects ought to be subject to remediation. What has been learned can be unlearned or altered. As a result of such thinking, behavioral training programs were established, using the then popular techniques, to change unwanted behaviors. When such programs were without noticeable success, the view was changed to hold that what was learned early in life was most important. Because it was learned so early in life, it was difficult to change. Accordingly, educational programs were established to work with children at very early ages. Preschool programs were stressed. Somewhat later Operation Headstart and other programs with catchy names were undertaken. Their results with culturally deprived children are subject to controversy, but they certainly have not led to any dramatic improvement in the abilities of the mentally deficient. This is not to say that the mentally deficient cannot profit from educational programs. Indeed, they stand in even greater need of education and training than those with normal intellectual capacities. But, the blank slate metaphor is misleading. No amount of early education can restore capacities lost because of abnormalities in brain development. And no amount of hope and desire will change that fact.

The Work Ethic

The Western World in general and the United States especially have accepted the work ethic which has derived, at least in part, from the Protestant ethic whereby a man gained salvation through hard work. His spiritual salvation was made obvious to others by the accumulation of wealth and possessions. The signs of heavenly grace were property and goods. As one became closer to the angels, prosperity and wealth were to abound. Hard work became essential to salvation and thus became valued both for its practical and spiritual consequences. Hence work becomes the goal of life.

Because mental deficiency often prohibits full or partial contributions to the work of society, it has been considered an abomination. Such thinking reached an extreme in

Germany under the Nazi regime when the mentally incompetent were exterminated. Not only were they considered a blight on Nazi society but also a source of malignancy that would poison future generations.

In past years mentally deficient people were banished to work farms. These were usually located in remote rural areas out of sight of the majority of the population. There they could till fields, harvest grain, work in simple occupations, and have their limited work potential utilized to the maximum. The ability to work was considered essential. Even today the institutional and community programs designed for the mentally deficient by professional educators, social workers, and therapists have as their most prominent objective the ability to obtain and hold a job.

Current Programs for the Mentally Deficient

How society views mentally deficient people determines what is done to and for them. When views are translated into action they are called *programs* and it is through such programs that the lives of the mentally deficient are enriched or depleted.

Society's views become programs and are implemented through the processes of legislation, appropriation, and delegation.

State and national legislatures enact laws and appropriate funds related to the mentally deficient. These laws are often broad in scope and correspondingly vague. They must be interpreted and implemented. These tasks fall to professional administrators in the state and federal bureaucracies. Many are dedicated and conscientious people, but as in every system, others are only adequate and a few less than that. It is useful to consider the entire group of administrators of the country's programs as an "establishment," that is, a group of people with an active and direct concern for programs directed toward mentally deficient people. There are professional associations and other groups that facilitate communication among them.

The Mental Retardation Establishments

The groups of administrators who interpret, implement, and monitor programs for the mentally deficient exist nationally, within states, within regions of states, and within institutions. The group of professional administrators of prominence within a state are relatively few and known by people in similar positions throughout the country. Spokesmen for this group of nationally known administrators represent a powerful lobby on the national scene. They also are influential in the states they represent.

81

Within regions of a state and within institutions a similar situation exists. Certain of the higher administrators represent their institutions to the state leadership and to the community. Without intention, perhaps, they have assumed the role of spokesmen for the employees serving under them.

These establishments play an important role in the development of programs for the mentally deficient. They develop their own ideas and plans for the mentally deficient. These ideas and plans reflect a uniformity and cohesion that comes from discussion among the members and a subsequent agreement among those involved. They are presented by the articulate spokesmen of the several establishments to people and groups influential in the legislative processes. They have access to those who have the decision-making power in government.

Many of the professional administrators are active or influential in national, statewide, and local groups organized to support the cause of the mentally deficient. These are associations which were established initially by parents to function as political lobbies. Typically, these organizations become so large that they must be run as businesses by professional administrators who have strong identification with other professional administrators in the state and federal bureaucracies.

As with many such groups, a minority of the members come to exert disproportionate influence. These are people with personal energy and drive. They are appointed to committees, become committee chairpersons and elected officials. The majority of the members do not become active participants. Since parents of mentally deficient persons come from all walks of life, a substantial number are far less educated than the professional administrators who become authority figures. In many instances, the opinions of the administrators are accepted unquestioningly by individual parents and parent groups.

In effect there are two major voices that influence the political scene: the establishments made up of the professional administrators and establishments composed of parents and similar groups who champion the cause of the mentally deficient.

While society, the public at large, may have views about the care and treatment of people with mental deficiencies, these are ill-formed and vague. Seldom are they expressed directly to those people and agencies that make decisions. Instead, it is the views of the mental retardation establishments that are made known to the decision makers. These views may or may not represent those held by the public-at-large or even by the majority of members of the bureaucracy. They may not even represent the feelings of parents in parent-groups since, as we noted above, the official opinions are forged by the few leaders of the groups.

The leaders of the various mental retardation establishments hold views that may not be those of their constituents. For those in the state and federal bureaucractic establishment, the constituents would be the employees of the governmental agencies involved with the care and treatment of the mentally handicapped. The needs of these public employees should be represented, but they are not identical with the needs of the mentally deficient, themselves. In principle, the parent groups would seem to be the most likely bodies to represent the needs of the mentally deficient. However, as mentioned, some of these parent groups have their opinions shaped by a minority who are leaders and professional administrators. Fads and trends in care and treatment may be established because of the politically active and vocal groups in the establishments. Only when there are wide discrepancies between current practices and views of society will there be a major "correction."

With these reservations about the breadth of popular support for programs and practices, it is now possible to consider some of the more prevalent views about the lives of the mentally deficient.

Normalization

One of the most popular principles underlying the approach of the retardation establishments is that of *normalization*. This concept is the basis of many of the major programs related to mental deficiency and it has received nationwide attention. According to this principle, the mentally deficient should live in the most "normal" setting possible. Implicit in this approach is the view that normal living conditions are those found in middle-class homes. The typical middle-class family is imagined to be like that of the Walton family on television. Few advocates of normalization suggest that Archie Bunker's home would be the ideal for a mentally deficient person.

Proponents of normalization seem to assume that most mentally deficient people would become more nearly normal in a middle-class home than in an institution. But since mental deficiency is a permanent affliction, not simply a delay in mental growth, a normal, middle-class home may be neither useful nor appropriate for a mentally deficient individual. Many normal homes may lead to hardship, pain, anxiety, and inappropriate types of behavior for a mentally deficient person.

The argument for normalization reeks of middle-class chauvinism. Opportunities are defined in terms of the desires, feelings, motives, and attitudes of the nonmentally deficient member of the middle-class. But what of the desires, feelings, and motives of the mentally deficient? Their values and goals may or may not correspond to the values and goals of nondeficient people. To assume that a mentally deficient person will achieve happiness in the same ways that a middle-class American does may not be appropriate.

The policy of normalization has its roots in the work ethic. In most habilitation programs written for mentally deficient individuals, one of the most prominent and clearly stated goals is to make the person a productive worker and taxpayer.

Deinstitutionalization

Over the past ten years, another trend of thought has become linked with the principle of normalization. This is the opinion that institutions for the mentally retarded are vile, evil places that stunt the already limited potentials of their residents. It is argued by the extremists that all institutions should therefore be closed in favor of community-based living. An associated position is that institutions for the mentally retarded should provide only temporary residence for the clients. It is sometimes said that if the appropriate training were given to mentally deficient individuals they could soon be productive contributors to society, hold jobs, pay taxes, and be integrated into normal community life. For the severely and profoundly retarded this is nonsense. It is an unrealistic denial of the fundamental nature of mental deficiency. The problem is that the mentally deficient will continue to be deficient. No amount of effort, training, education, or habilitation will alter this basic fact. Considering mental deficieny a temporary phenomenon obscures the permanent nature of the difficulty.

One of the practical problems concerning present plans for deinstitutionalization of the mentally deficient is that most programs are simply directed toward getting people out of the institutions. Getting the person into an adequate school setting, a reasonable vocational rehabilitation program, a sheltered workshop, an opportunity center, or a job are sometimes secondary to just getting the person out. But even if these community-based programs are available, planning must not end here. What kind of a life will the individual have after school days are over, after the vocational training has ended, or after gainful employment is terminated?

Studies of mentally deficient people living in communities after release from institutions reveal a bleak and meager outlook. They live in the lowest ranges of the socioeconomic scale, without hope of significant advancement in terms of jobs or income.

In one group home for the mentally deficient, I met a young man of about twentyfive years of age who was released from the institution because he had obtained employment as dishwasher in a rundown cafe. This man was fired from his job after a couple of weeks because he was frequently late and sometimes did not show up for work. He also did not clean the dishes very well. In the next six months he only was able to work about two weeks at miscellaneous, temporary jobs. He had no educational, vocational, or recreational activities and spent most of his time panhandling change in the bus terminal. Yet, this young man had a bed and some food provided by the group living home to which he had been assigned. In this way he was better off than similar mentally deficient persons who end up living a hand-to-mouth existence, sleeping in parks or abandoned buildings.

Programs whose goals do not extend beyond getting a job or with the completion of an educational program are insufficient. Plans for the mentally deficient cannot end five or even ten years in the future. Any comprehensive program must consider the total abilities and potentialities of the individual in society from the time of early adulthood through maturity and old age. Without programs designed for *life*, a movement toward deinstitutionalization is premature.

Motives Behind Deinstitutionalization

The current emphasis on the release of mentally deficient people from institutions stems from several motives. One is the position that institutions are evil by their very nature and that they will aggravate the behavioral deficiencies already troubling the person. It is argued that institutions cannot provide the normal environment deemed essential by proponents of normalization.

Other arguments are of a more practical nature. Some are based on the belief that institutions with hundreds or a thousand or more people are just too difficult to manage. The alternative of having small institutions is held to be uneconomical since there would be many duplications of services and support facilities. Since large institutions are hard to manage and small ones inefficient, the argument is made that there should not be any!

Another practical argument is based on money. The costs of keeping one person in an institution with decent facilities and programs total over ten thousand dollars per year. Because of the number of people now in institutions, that cost is a heavy tax burden. For example, in the state of Florida, there are about 6,000 people in institutions for the mentally deficient. In New York, the number is about 40,000. This means that the cost of care, programs, and services amounts to about 62 million dollars a year in Florida and 600 million in New York for just the clients living in institutions. The costs of buildings, renovations, furnishings, care and treatment for all mentally deficient in Florida amount to 100 million dollars a year. The total cost for the United States is about 11 billion dollars per year, an impressive figure.*

Most state legislatures appropriate less than is needed for mentally deficient people living in institutions. And the care and programs provided are accordingly inadequate. Many specialists and legislators believe that people can be maintained in foster and group

*The data about Florida and National expenditures were given to me by Mr. Francis Kelly, Program Director, Retardation Division, Department of Health and Rehabilitative Services, State of Florida.

homes for less than the cost of living in an institution. Superficially, it seems that a substantial savings for state and federal governments could be achieved by placing as many mentally deficient people in group and foster homes as possible.

But the savings may be more apparent than real. First, the majority of clients in institutions are usually not those who can maintain themselves in an independent or even semi-independent fashion. The majority of institutionalized clients are severely and profoundly deficient, often with other medical or physical problems. Such people require more care, supervision, and special equipment than can be given in a group living home. For those capable of living in less structured circumstances, nursing care, medical and dental costs, education, rehabilitation programs, recreational activities, and the like cost money over and beyond the amount spent for room and board. It is quite possible that these additional costs for mentally deficient people living in group or foster homes could exceed the costs of the same people living in a good institution. The main difference is the budgetary pocket from which the funds come. The administrators of state bureaucracies appear in the best light to their legislatures when they seem to be operating efficiently on small budgets. Deinstitutionalization produces this effect by shifting the source of funds from state or national treasuries to local sources. There is no net benefit to the taxpayer. If full accountability could be established for the cost of maintaining a moderately or severely mentally deficient person in an institution or in a group or foster home, it would probably become apparent that there is no significant difference between them.

What Kinds of People are in Institutions?

In recent years there have been many types of support offered to families with mentally deficient children. These include respite care, preschool programs, special education programs, and sheltered workshops. The net effect of these new directions of support has been to reduce the demand for institutionalization of children with mild or even moderate mental deficiencies. As a result, the majority of residents now in institutions have moderate, severe, or profound levels of mental deficiency. Many have additional handicaps, such as cerebral palsy, epilepsy, sensory impairments, metabolic disorders, and other physical problems. Clearly today there is an ever-decreasing number of clients in institutions who have the abilities necessary for independent or even semi-independent life.

Criteria for Deinstitutionalization

The first priority for the transfer of people from institutions to foster and group home settings should be those who should not be in the institution at all. In years past many people were committed to institutions for the mentally deficient for reasons other than mental deficiency, including criminal acts and emotional disorders. Some were placed there as an alternative to an orphanage. These misplaced groups should be the first to leave the institutions. Their presence there is harmful both to the institution and to themselves, since their own treatment or habilitation programs are inadequate. If properly treated, they would be able to lead lives indistinguishable from those led by people of the same educational and social backgrounds. The programs leading to their placement in the community should be educational and vocational to provide them with competitive skills in the job market. For these people, normalization makes sense.

The second class of residents to consider for release to group and foster homes would be those with the greatest intellectual capacities. One should note, however, that intellectual abilities are not all of a piece. Many individuals with below normal IQ will have certain skills and talents well within the normal range. These mildly and moderately retarded individuals deserve a chance to find out *if* they can function in a reasonable manner in society. For them, training in vocational and social skills (in the broadest sense) should be provided, and their individual talents developed. They should be given an opportunity for group or foster home placement, and then supervised living in an apartment or other domicile. Some of them may be able to lead almost independent lives. Others may not. Therefore, it seems obvious that alternatives with widely differing amounts of supervision and support should be provided. Provisions also must be made for these persons to drop back into a more secure and ordered existence if they prove unable to live without supervision.

For both of these categories of clients, programs with increasingly independent living should be undertaken as soon as possible. There is little doubt that life in many institutions can erode exactly those abilities needed to get along in society. On the other hand, a moderately deficient individual may *not* be well served by being placed in a foster home setting, if specialized training to enhance his or her particular skills is not available there. A foster or group home, in and of itself, does not guarantee that the individual will become prepared to assume a reasonably independent existence. Specialized vocational or educational training may be more readily available in an institution than out in the community.

Those for whom group or foster home placement would be least advisable are those individuals who have little or no chance of being able to survive in any but a highly supervised environment. The intellectual shortcomings of many of the mentally deficient are so great that even with some special abilities they will not be able to cope with society. They will not be able to deal with such matters as shopping, insurance, health care, nor, in general, to assume responsibility for their actions. These people must be closely supervised.

Other Factors Pertaining to Deinstitutionalization

Beyond these considerations there are still others pertaining to the selection of clients for placement in group or foster homes. For adult clients who are capable of making decisions their own desires should be considered. Certain moderately deficient people may wish to leave the institution while others may not.

Operators of group homes for the mentally deficient consistently report that those who wanted to leave the institution and live in group homes usually made a success of it. On the other hand, clients who did not wish to give up their friends or the structured environment of the institution were unhappy outside and soon had to be returned to the institution. Hence, even on a practical basis the desire of people to live in a group or foster home and to try to live independently must be considered.

In the case of clients whose mental deficiencies are greater, one cannot place the same degree of reliance on the individual's ability to report his or her desires. Often communication skills are inadequate to gain understanding of the person's feelings. The individual may be unable to comprehend alternatives. Who can best speak for the feelings or the benefit of the more severely deficient individual? Some authorities maintain that the parents are not the best judges of what is appropriate for their child, and that specialists in mental deficiency, usually working for a state agency, are better able to do so than the parents. But despite the burdens carried by most parents of deficient children, they are dedicated to obtaining the best possible circumstances for their child. Their thoughts and desires are singularly directed toward actions and procedures which will benefit the child. They have a long-term perspective. It is not a question of what will happen this year or next, but what will happen five and ten years from now. Parents are concerned with the quality of their children's total lives. Therefore, in the case of both moderately retarded minors with some hope of independent life and all mentally deficient individuals with severe intellectual impairment, the parents' views should be paramount. In addition, without the parents' active support and assistance, placements into group or foster homes are not going to be beneficial.

For mentally deficient individuals who do not have parents to make such a decision, guardians or court-appointed representatives must take the place of the parents in the decision-making process. Despite the difficulties of this procedure there is no other option that genuinely safeguards the interests of the mentally deficient.

Quite often parents of mentally deficient children are unwilling, or at least reluctant, to approve placement of their child in foster or group homes. At times this seems unrealistic to professional administrators. To the social worker, the placement of the child in a pleasant foster home or well-run group living home represents an obvious improvement on the conditions found in an "evil" institution. The disapproval of the placement by the parents seems arbitrary and cruel.

However, as mentioned earlier, the parents view their child's infirmity in the long term. Often the view of the professional is more immediate. "Here is a nice place. Here is a nice child. Let's put them together." The parents' view might well recognize the pleasantness of the surroundings provided by a group or foster home but ask the additional questions: How long will the home be in good condition? Are the foster parents old or young? If old, questions as to the health of the foster parents become important. How long will they be able to take care of the foster children? If the foster parents are young, the question might be how long will it be before the couple wishes to have their own children? How will the birth of natural children in the future affect the care of the foster children? Will the interests of the young couple change over time? Will they move away? What will happen then?

A prime consideration of the parents is the stability and permanency of the arrangement. While they recognize that a given group or foster home setting may be useful at one time they are concerned over the temporary nature of the arrangement. They are concerned about what will happen if conditions in the foster or group home deteriorate and the child has to be returned to the institution or placed elsewhere.

Other considerations also influence the parents' concerns over and beyond the physical nature of the group or foster home, and the personalities of the group/foster home parents. These include the training and educational programs available in the community, medical and dental care, and opportunities for a productive and interesting life for the child.

Summary

This chapter began with what mentally deficient people are not. They are not perpetual children.

They are not from, or suited to, a different culture.

They are not only handicapped in school, they are handicapped in all aspects of society and this is reflected in a decreased ability to work. Because of the work ethic this has importance beyond the failure to contribute to the products of society. Work is a goal with moral as well as practical implications, and most programs for the mentally deficient list the capacity to achieve and maintain employment in a high priority position.

Programs for the mentally deficient come about through legislation and through the implementation of laws by state and federal bureaucracies. The laws and their implementation are not direct reflections of the views of society but of the mental retardation establishments. Their goals are not identical with the needs of the mentally handicapped. Two recently emphasized goals are normalization and deinstitutionalization. These goals are motivated, in part, by the view that it would cost less to care for a mentally deficient person in the community than in an institution. This may be illusory. In any case, many mentally deficient will need institutional care for many years, while others are probably able to live less supervised lives outside of institutions. Parents are greatly concerned about the consistency and permanence of living conditions for their mentally deficient children. This concern is often not shared by professional administrators whose interest is primarily in decreasing the number of mentally deficient in institutions.

FIVE

Problems of the
Mentally Deficient

Because of the behavioral difficulties of the mentally deficient even the mildly deficient person faces a variety of special problems. In this chapter I shall discuss three types of problems: Education, emotional disturbances, and sexual behavior. We shall be looking at the way things are now and begin the consideration of the way they could be in the future. The shape of that future will be the principal topic of Chapter Six.

Education

The altered behavioral capacities of the mentally deficient have profound effects on the ability to master the "three Rs" on which academic success is built. Without "Reading, 'Riting, and 'Rithmetic," little progress is possible within the educational system or within society. Because there are so many people with educational problems, including the mentally deficient, *special* education has been developed to cope with those problems. The basic notion is to produce training in educational skills for those with less than usual academic capacities. The nature and quality of special education programs depend on the thinking of the school system and the resources of the community. But, good or bad, special education is geared to a very heterogeneous population. For example, it is intended to provide some modicum of ed-

102

ucation to those who are handicapped by specific disabilities (e.g., those with reading problems but who otherwise are bright), those who are somewhat below average in ability, those with environmental disadvantages who are moving ahead too slowly in regular classes, those with emotional disturbances, and those more generally handicapped—the mentally deficient.

The problems of local school boards are increasing as more and more children with educational difficulties enter the school system. In many states, legislation makes it mandatory for school systems to accept children with *all* levels of mental abilities. To serve these children it has become necessary to add additional programs and teachers. A vocationally oriented program suited for a person with only slightly reduced mental potential would be quite different from the training suited to a severely deficient person. The goals, teaching methods, and materials would all be different.

The ability to learn and to progress within a school system does not depend on measured IQ alone. People with the same IQ scores may have different abilities to acquire and retain information. A person who learns too slowly and forgets too rapidly should be treated quite differently than one who learns too rapidly but forgets too slowly. The ability of the person to focus attention, to restrain impulses that interefere with learning, and to have an attentive attitude for a prolonged period of time must also be taken into consideration. But to base educational programs on these considerations is impossible at this time because (1) individualized evaluations and *meaningful* teaching plans cannot be made for every student, and (2) even if these could be done it would not be economically feasible for already overburdened school boards to undertake such programs.

On the first point, it is impossible to prepare effective educational programs for individualized special education students for several reasons. There are no standard tests for the various behavioral capacities other than IQ Rates of learning, forgetting, personal interests, impulse-control, attention span and the like are not subject to common measurement procedures and even if standardized tests were devised, we know very little about what corrective procedures would be most successful. This means that the learning capacities and behavior of each person must be evaluated on an individual basis by competent and enlightened professionals who can spend the time and energy required to make appropriate evaluations and recommendations. There just are not enough professional people with adequate training around to do the job for the large number of people with learning handicaps.

On the second point, school systems of most American communities are already overburdened to the point that new programs or projects are unlikely to be initiated. To do an adequate job of special education for present students who need this service is already beyond capacity of most school boards. Moreover, present tax burdens are so great that any further increase for use of the school systems is politically impossible. Therefore, even if diagnostic services were available, their cost would be prohibitive.

The slogan that all children are entitled to an education is beautiful, but many of the moderately, severely, and profoundly deficient cannot profit from education in the usual sense of the word. They can profit from training. They can also come to appreciate new activities and experiences. Many can learn relatively simple skills. But should this sort of training be provided by school boards? This is a fundamental question and can only be discussed in the context of what the life of mentally deficient persons should be like.

In accepting the principle of normalization, many people have also accepted as fact that the special education programs now in existence in the public schools would be suitable for the moderate to profoundly deficient.

Separated, specialized educational programs for the mentally deficient have not been developed and it is questionable that they will be in the near future. The public school programs remain the only viable educational programs for the mentally deficient despite their practical limitations. However, the goals of their programs should be considered in terms of the prospects of the mentally handicapped for their long-term goals in life. It is this aspect of the educational programs that can be altered and improved in the near future. Certain of the proposals in the next chapter bear on this matter.

Mental Illness

Being mentally deficient does not provide protection against emotional or behavioral disorders. In fact, it may even predispose people toward emotional disturbances. The mentally handicapped are especially prone to insecurity and anxiety because of a greater vulnerability to the stresses of the environment. They are limited in their abilities to form abstractions, to use language and symbols effectively, and to use imagination. Some psychiatrists have arrived at the general conclusion that all mentally deficient people have immature personalities and poor differentiation of "ego structure." As a person with limited capacities is exposed to the difficulties of life and to a series of events in which failure is likely, personality defenses may be used more and more frequently. In the usual public school setting failure is especially likely because the behavioral capacities of the mentally deficient are different from those of the others in special education programs and the limited physical capacities of the mentally deficient handicap them even during play and recreation.

Some of the emotional disorders of the mentally deficient may be qualitatively different from those found in nondeficient populations. What is being done for mentally deficient individuals with emotional problems? What should be done?

The major emphasis in therapy for emotional disturbances is on modifications of the psychoanalytic theories developed early in this century by Sigmund Freud. In this approach the personality is thought to be the product of basic biological urges and their method of expression through opportunities presented in the environment. When the basic urges are not sufficiently gratified, or are overly indulged, personality development is abnormal. Therapeutic measures involve using dialogue between the patient and the therapist to uncover periods in which the basic urges of the individual received inappropriate gratification. This allows the patient to understand the nature of the disturbance as well as permitting the patient to relive some of the emotions experienced in the past.

The technique depends on the verbal exchange between the client and the therapist. At times this exchange requires a high degree of verbal sophistication. As a therapeutic technique, it is most successful with highly verbal and educated people. The less verbal the person, the less successful is this technique. This great dependence on verbal exchange makes it poorly suited for use with the mentally deficient who have trouble with subtle expressions even if they have basic language skills.

Consequently, the basic psychoanalytic approach has seldom been tried with mentally defective people. Not only is it inappropriate and ill-suited to their abilities, but it is an expensive technique requiring a prolonged period of discussion between patient and therapist on a one-to-one basis. Disregarding the cost of the treatment, there just are not enough psychoanalytically trained psychiatrists and psychologists available to fill the potential needs of the mentally deficient. Therefore, other techniques that depend less on verbal skills have been applied to the troubles of the mentally deficient.

Reality Therapy

Reality therapy is an approach developed by Dr. William Glasser, a California psychiatrist, who, along with Dr. G. L. Harrington, became convinced that more traditional models of psychotherapy were inappropriate to the needs of many young clients, especially those having difficulties in coping with school or with the rules of society more generally. (See W. Glasser, *Reality Therapy*. New York: Harper and Row, 1965.) Glasser felt that certain general principles of therapy could be applied to many types of behavioral disturbances. He also deemphasized the importance of probing the patient's past to uncover the causes of behavioral problems. In fact, he even doubted that a person needed to have insight into his mental processes for behavioral change to occur. This aspect made it seem appropriate for mentally deficient individuals. Glasser emphasized the need for the evaluation of behavior by others and to teach people better, more acceptable ways of acting.

In *Reality Therapy*, Glasser tried to develop ways in which people could be led to face their environment and to accept the idea that they are responsible for their own acts.

Patients are urged to make their own evaluations of their actions.

Glasser holds that in institutional settings the therapist should point out the effects of particular behavior for the individual because of reactions of the institution's administrators and other residents.

Special rewards are arranged for actions of particular residents. They are told "If you do *this*, then *that* will happen to you." A resident might be told after destroying a chair when angry, "If you break up furniture again, you will be transferred to a cottage with less freedom." Another person prone to using foul language might be instructed: "If you keep saying abusive things, your privilege of visiting the canteen will be revoked."

Sometimes reality therapy is applied in groups in which several residents exchange information. One resident might describe how the behavior of another makes him feel or act. Guided by a skillful leader, this group approach can be used to provide all of the participants with a sharper view of their present circumstances. The group sessions provide useful information about how one person's behavior influences others that might otherwise not be readily detected.

Therapeutic programs based on reality therapy were first applied in a California detention facility for girls who had been convicted of crimes, some of a major nature. All aspects of life at the institution were aimed at making each resident aware of her own responsibilities with the continued support of a warm personal relationship with the therapist.

Such a relationship is a key in reality therapy. The need is for someone who can be relied on. As Glasser points out: "The ability to get involved is the major skill of doing reality therapy. . . ." This emphasis on involvement and a continuing long-term commitment to the patient also points out one of the major difficulties of reality therapy approaches as they are implemented in many institutions.

Reality therapy is often undertaken in institutions where treatment sessions are isolated events, ones which are not part of the total program of the institution. Often a leader of a reality therapy group is at the institution or a group living home only for a few sessions held each week.

Since the therapy experience and the therapist are not part of the daily lives of the residents, the lessons learned in the sessions may not be supported and reinforced. A consistent external reality and approach to activities is essential to the success of the approach. Without it, the therapy becomes a game played at certain times of the week but not relevant at other times.

The problem is compounded by the high rate of turnover among professional staffs in most state or federal institutions. Different therapists often substitute for each other in guiding the sessions. This leads to a lack of consistency. More important, however, is the fact that this inconsistency makes it difficult for the therapist to become involved with any participant. Hence the very cornerstone of the process is impaired. With conditions of high staff turnover and frequent substitutions among therapists, residents will not be able to accept sincerity and involvement of those trying to help them.

The establishment of reality therapy programs for residents in institutions for the mentally deficient have all of the difficulties mentioned above and some additional ones besides. First among these would be the fact that the reality of the mentally deficient person may be quite different from that of the nondeficient. This stems from different capabilities and different perspectives. In group treatment, the composition of the group may be quite diverse in terms of the participants' mental abilities. Moreover, the goal of reality therapy is to enable the individual to form a realistic and responsible plan for his or her own actions, and it is in just this domain that the mentally deficient person is most handicapped.

Furthermore, the selective use of rewards and deprivations to show clients the effect of their actions in reality is really but one form of behavioral modification programs to be described in the next section. It differs from behavior modification by requiring the client's understanding of verbal descriptions of contingencies of behavior and the anticipation of future rewards and punishments. Because of this, it would be suitable only for the mentally deficient people whose ability to anticipate the future is intact. It would be of no use for the moderately to severely deficient.

Behavior Modification

Behavior modification is a technique used to change specific behaviors. It follows the principles developed by Professor B. F. Skinner of Harvard University. In this approach, behavior is altered by the application of reinforcements or reinforcers just after the response that is to be altered has occurred. Skinner advocates the rejection of complicated and involved theories of behavior in favor of the intensive study of changes in an individual's behavior after the application of reinforcements. (A reinforcement is defined as a stimulus or an event that changes an individual's behavior.) A pat on

113

the back or a message of congratulations may act as a reinforcer. When we give a young boy a piece of candy or a toy after he does something we want him to, these can be called reinforcers. From this point of view, educators and others interested in changing behavior must find circumstances and procedures that act as reinforcers if they wish to mold behavior.

Another aspect of the behavior modification approach is the intensive study of one individual. This means that the circumstances and conditions under which a particular behavior occurs must be carefully studied. Once the behaviors occurring in a situation are understood, then it is possible to attempt a new program of applying reinforcers so that the behavior becomes modified. For example, parents might be concerned about a child who shouts and screams in the home. A therapist with a behavior modification approach would look carefully at what happened just before each episode and at the responses elicited from parents or others in the child's immediate environment after each bout. Perhaps screaming occurs every time the mother ignores the child. The screaming terminates when the mother comes in and picks up the child. It is important to know both the stimuli that come before the particular behavior and the effects produced by the behavior. In our example screaming was reinforced by being picked up and held. Changing the behavior requires changing the consequences (reinforcements) it produces.

The behavior modification approach does not require anticipation of future rewards or punishments. It does not require sophisticated language ability. A particular behavior occurs and immediately a reinforcement, either positive or negative, is applied with consistency. Because of the fact that neither the ability to imagine future contingencies or high verbal skills are needed, behavior modification oftens works exceptionally well with the mentally deficient.

However, the appropriate use of behavior modification techniques requires a great deal of training and experience. It is not something that can be simply undertaken. Specific courses and training programs are necessary in order to become competent in the procedures. Using the procedures appropriately, a large number of successes have been reported from the application of the principles of behavior modification to specific behaviors of mentally deficient people. These include the enhancement of desirable behaviors and the elimination of unwanted acts. Examples of these unwanted behaviors cover a wide range of activities: not eating certain foods, not sitting at the table during dinner, screaming, crying, bedwetting, and unacceptable social behaviors. As long as the behavior is specific enough to be observed, it can be changed through the appropriate application of reinforcements. Many school and preschool programs are now modifying behavior through this technique. Some schools are applying behavior modification techniques in the classroom.

To be maximally effective behavior modification programs must be coordinated in all circumstances of the person's life. Parents, teachers, trainers, and others must come to understand the principles of behavior modification and how to apply them to specific behaviors. Behavior modification is not a panacea for all behavioral problems. There is no doubt that it is an effective procedure for altering some specific behaviors. Nevertheless, it is usually the case that the major problem is not one specific behavior but a large variety of behaviors. Behavior modification can only be applied to one particular behavior through a consistent reinforcement program. To be sure, once one behavioral act comes under control, then it is possible to move on to change another. But gaining control of even a single unwanted behavior requires time. The application of behavior modification techniques require a consistent and deliberate approach in which the appropriate reinforcement is applied uniformly after each and every response. The elimination of an undesirable response may take weeks or even longer. Nevertheless, it does work given the determination of those around the person to make it work.

Why do behavior modification techniques often work better with the mentally handicapped than with the nonhandicapped? The answer may be that some mentally deficient are capable of rapid learning of simple responses, those probably formed on the basis of mechanisms of the R-complex of the brain. With the reduction of effectiveness of the neocortical systems that are closely associated with fantasy and imagination, there is less likelihood of experimentation and testing of reinforcement contingencies being imposed. As a result, the behaviors of some of the mentally deficient are modified easily and tend to stay modified longer.

The Humanistic Approach

The humanistic movement in psychology is relatively new, as a movement, although it has a long established basis in existential philosophy and in some forms of psychotherapy. Its basic assumption is that a person is free and responsible for his or her actions. It emphasizes the actualization of the capacities of each person and strives to achieve a reduction in barriers that interfere with communication among people. As a corollary, it advocates a reduction of dependence on old, established behavioral patterns so that new experiences can be obtained and new techniques developed for coping with the world.

Facilitating Communication

There are several possible applications of the humanistic approach that could be applied to mentally deficient individuals. The first of these pertains to how communication can be increased among mentally deficient individuals and, further, between them and nondeficient people.

Probably the most remarkable example of the importance of communication was among profoundly deficient people in an institution in the State of Washington.* At this institution one ward held a rather large number of residents isolated from one another by their profound mental deficiencies and by their physical abnormalities as well. All of these residents had some form of cerebral palsy and were usually lying in different positions, the nature of which was dictated by the particular pattern of retraction of their muscles. They were mostly unresponsive to

---

*Personal observations of Dr. Eugene Sackett, 1974.

118

nurses and attendants. Few, if any, ever uttered a sound. They did not try to communicate with other residents, either while in bed or when placed on the floor during various attempts at physical therapy. As an experiment, some of the staff tried placing the residents in highly moldable bean-bag chairs in positions that would facilitate breathing. Many of the residents had great trouble breathing when on a nearly flat surface. When placed in positions near each other on the floor their main concern was to overcome difficulties in respiration. By using bean-bag chairs, positions could be achieved so each client could be comfortable.

These clients also had difficulties in making physical contact with each other since their arms and hands were greatly disformed by muscle retractions produced by the disease. Therefore, the residents were arranged in bean-bag chairs so that they could touch each other, if they wanted, with their feet. They began to do so and thus established some human contacts which had been impossible for them previously.

The surprising consequence of this interaction was that the residents began to become more responsive to the nurses and attendants. Verbal communication increased and one patient, previously thought to be mute, suddenly began to expressing himself

119

with well-formed sentences. Apparently, this client had far greater intellectual abilities than had been imagined. The inability to establish contact with others had made him unable or unwilling to express them.

The problems of communication with profoundly and moderately deficient individuals are not easily overcome. Many such people have severe speech problems that hide and obscure higher level abilities. Since speech is such an important part of human existence, speech therapy should be an important part of all programs for the mentally deficient.

But people do not communicate entirely by speech or verbal communication. There are forms of communications which involve signs and symbolic acts. There is a language of the body, of facial expressions, of gestures. People who cannot speak because of problems of articulation can learn sign languages. People can become sensitive to gestures, motions, and small movements of the facial muscles. The touch of a hand or of a foot can convey a great deal of meaning. The ways we touch or do not touch someone else expresses our feelings far better than words. Even profoundly deficient people use bodies to talk. An important avenue of investigation would be to determine just how they do and what their body vocabulary is like.

Developing Abilities

Humanistically oriented therapists believe that many forms of mental disease stem from the acceptance of traditional ways of living which do not allow for personal growth and development. They go beyond reality therapy by saying that while each person is responsible for his or her actions, they are also responsible for their own growth and development.

This message can be translated into actions and programs for the mentally deficient: Find out the abilities, capacities, and interests of the individual and then help to develop them fully. Every mentally deficient person carries with him a particular combination of abilities, interests, and desires. Too often programs for the mentally deficient are designed to produce persons geared to cope with the world as it exists for the nondeficient. Since there are many areas in which the mentally deficient individual will not show great development, broad goals suitable for all are not realistic.

Many of the emotional problems of the mentally deficient stem from inappropriate programs and plans for them. Aggressive acts of mentally deficient people are often associated with their assignment to inappropriate programs in institutions. When a person is fulfilling him or herself, the need for self-expression in violence lessens.

Recently I reviewed the suggestions made by the late Sidney Jourard in his book *The Healthy Personality*,* that were aimed at helping people grow in their own abilities and capacities. Following his approach, the first thing that must be done is to believe that the mentally deficient do have capacities that can be enhanced. Then other questions must be asked: "What changes can be made for greater personal growth?" "What prevents them from growing?" If it is believed that a mentally deficient individual can be a good artist, musician, radio repairman, or whatever, believing is half of the battle.

Just like the nondeficient individual, the person with limited capacities often hesitates to begin new efforts. Primarily it is concern over venturing into new worlds when the present one may not be under control. There is always the possibility of additional failure, and if the penalty for failure appears to be great, so will the hesitancy in beginning. To make new ventures the mentally deficient individual must be made to feel valued and worthy. With such feelings, failures will not produce permanent effects.

---

*Sidney M. Jourard, *The Healthy Personality* (New York: Macmillan, 1974).

Many mentally adequate people need help in beginning new ways of life. "Growth centers" have sprung up around the United States to help people change. Diets and fasting, meditation, Yoga and Rolfing are employed to assist people break with old, unrewarding ways of life. It is not unreasonable that similar types of experiences may help the mentally deficient to try new things in order to explore their full potentialities. If it is hard for the nondeficient to explore new ways of doing things, how much harder must it be for those with less than full mental abilities!

Enhancing Self-Image

Each of us believes certain things to be true about him- or herself. How accurate are these observations? Jourard suggested that people look at themselves and at others carefully. He admonished people to be careful what they think about themselves, because their beliefs are likely to become self-fulfilling prophecies. One of the important services that can be done for the mentally deficient is to make sure that they have favorable views of themselves.

A person's image in a mirror or in the eyes of others is important. To be sure, the image is not the person. Still, it would be difficult for anyone in drab prison garb to have a high self-evaluation. In this day of television and mass communication, styles of dress and grooming are widespread symbols of personal value. Therefore it is important for the people living in institutions or group homes to see themselves looking as good as they can. For those with obvious physical deformities, everyone working with them should be encouraged to find the best ways to make them be and feel more attractive. The advice of associates should be solicited. Becoming attractive is more than a game, it is a matter of making life worth living.

The mentally handicapped must be convinced that they are valuable to others and to the society or group in which they live. They should feel appreciated by others. This is one of the reasons that communication among mentally deficient individuals is so important. Many times it is the companionship, mutual entertainment, and amusement afforded by a peer group of other mentally deficient individuals from which the greatest source of self-appreciation can be obtained. If one individual has a talent for music, another for drawing, another for dancing, and another for telling stories, each make their contributions and profit in turn from the admiration of other people in the group. The same thing applies to sports. Many of the mentally deficient can participate in competitive sports to a limited extent. When individuals become relatively successful in basketball, softball, track, or other sports, they gain a way of viewing themselves in a favorable light. If a person exhibits a talent for a sport, this should be encouraged just as any other form of special talent. It does not matter if the sport is wheelchair basketball or baseball for the blind. It is being on a team and the working with others that counts.

We must recognize that many of the ways in which nondeficient individuals find status and self-satisfaction are going to be denied to the mentally deficient. These include success in education and business. Therefore successes outside of the educational system and employment must be emphasized.

At times everyone becomes tired and bored with his present circumstances. When people become dispirited through boredom, a change is needed. The same thing applies to the mentally deficient. For those whose lives must be led within an institution, boredom is a too frequent companion. This suggests that changes of cottages, of schools, of types of training, should be possible. The residents ought to be allowed vacations, camping trips, visits to parks, as a matter of established routine. Change encourages growth. During periods of change individuals may well find that they have new talents and abilities and with such discoveries there will be new desires to express these newly found talents.

All of us are afraid of certain situations or some people. Sometimes one particular situation is especially threatening to us. Educational programs ought to include training in acceptable ways of dealing with such situations and people as well as teaching ways to exhibit emotion without harming others.

One way of doing this is to encourage the use of role-playing techniques with the mildly or moderately deficient. For those capable of doing so, it would be valuable to have them play extemporaneous skits in which one assumes the role of an employee and another the role of a client. Four or five mentally deficient people could be involved. This would allow them to express their feelings about supervisors or about other residents. At the same time, emotions could be exhibited which might be awkward or harmful if expressed directly. Role playing can also serve to establish communication between residents and employees.

Participating in Decision Making

Not only do people feel valued because of their appearance or their talents, they also feel valued when their opinions and thoughts are taken into consideration. If no one listens to you, you come to believe that what you say

126

is of no importance. Residents in all types of living situations should have an active role in determining their daily regimes. Even the more severely handicapped residents have opinions about matters which concern them. Although it may be time-consuming and difficult, the opinions of the mentally deficient should be solicited and, where possible, used as a basis for change in daily regimes or policies. Extending the matter, clients' interests should be represented in the organization of institutions. Delegates and representatives should be elected by the members of living units and serve as advisors to the administrators. Where communication handicaps render such election and representation impossible, volunteer advocates may have to serve as the representatives of the interests of residents. For advocates to represent residents' interest, they must take the time to learn what the residents want and need. Mentally deficient people need to know that their needs and desires are not forgotten even when they cannot communicate them in the normal fashion.

In institutions, residents, their representatives, and advocates should be involved in establishing rules of discipline for the living units. Disciplinary actions are obviously necessary for acts that are disruptive or cause injury to others, but who is best able to decide on appropriate disciplinary action? One reasonable answer is: Those who are most affected by the misbehavior. Beyond this, the participation of residents in the establishment of disciplinary procedures serves to enhance the self-perception of every person involved.

Similarly, residents need to participate in determining what sort of jobs they should have in the living unit or in the institution. No one, deficient or nondeficient, wants to be told in an arbitrary fashion that *this* is your job. The desires and capabilities of the individual must be taken into account, and changes in occupations are to be expected and encouraged. People should try different sorts of jobs from time to time to see which ones provide them the greatest satisfaction.

Room to Grow

Privacy is something all people want and need. As with all people, there are times to be with others and times to be alone. A nonretarded individual can be alone on a quiet beach, on a walk in the woods, or sitting quietly in a secluded place and reading. Unfortunately, many of the mentally deficient individuals are handicapped in reading and substitutes for this form of being alone must be found. For some, puzzles or games would be useful. Music and working with clay or paints could provide an individual activity. Privacy is probably the most difficult thing to obtain for the mentally deficient person living in an institution or group-living home.

The approach of humanistically-oriented therapists, like Jourard, is based on consideration of how the patient's life has become unlivable. It examines all of the ways in which people have become less than they could be. Freedom to live and to grow in many aspects of life are essential to a healthy personality. This freedom is usually denied the mentally deficient to a much greater extent than necessary.

Another aspect of a complete life is the domain of love. Love can be thought of as a commitment to the well-being of another person. It engenders some of the finest emotions, going well beyond physical attractiveness and physical acts of sex. For the mentally deficient individual in the institution and in the community, both love and sexual expression present difficult problems.

Feelings of affection between the mentally and physically handicapped may be expressed in many ways. Charming and poignant demonstrations of affection can be seen in all group-living homes and institutions where men and women, boys and girls, are allowed to be with each other. Hands are held, shoulders are touched, contact with feet or other extremities are seen. Having a friend, a companion, regardless of sex is important to all people. Much too often, the public becomes alarmed that contact between the sexes is dangerous because of the possibility of physical sexual acts occurring. The question of sexual relations *per se* is not the point. Most reports from group-living homes and institutions where relatively free interactions are permitted between men and women indicate that the incidence of physical sexuality is much rarer than would be expected on the basis of the intermingling of similar members of nondeficient individuals.

Sex and Sex Education

Because of society's reluctance to discuss sexual matters, both the physiological basis of reproduction and information about sexual behaviors have been neglected in training programs for the mentally deficient. This neglect has occurred despite the fact that the mentally deficient have a great need for such training. This greater need for sex education arises from the fact that the mentally deficient are less likely to obtain useful information from books, magazines, motion pictures, television, and their associates than are nondeficient people.

The need for sex education is real and recognized by most parents, educators, and administrators, for despite the lower frequency of sex acts among the mentally deficient some sexual activities do occur in all institutions or group-living facilities, no matter how closely the residents are supervised or how stringently separated.

Sexual acts among the mentally deficient take all the forms found in society at large: masturbation, heterosexual, homosexual, and group sex. In institutions there will also be prostitution and rape, both heterosexual and homosexual. It is no use to pretend such things do not or will not happen. They will and they do. They happen inside and outside of institutions and this must be recognized from the start.

As mentioned before, the differences between the brains of a mentally deficient and a normal individual are in those structures and systems last to develop. The anatomical and hormonal basis for sexual behaviors are located in the neural systems earliest to form, those of the R-complex, and for many, if not most, mentally deficient people, their reproductive equipment functions in a nearly normal fashion. Interruptions of the neural systems controlling reproductive acts would require that the brain damage would have to have occurred at such an early gestational age and to be so severe that the fetus would fail to survive.

The ability to reproduce is, in this sense, a capacity highly protected from developmental disasters.

To educate is to inform. If the mentally deficient person is to be educated, he or she must be given information about the physiological apparatus necessary for sex, its meaning, significance, and consequences. However, there is a difference between education and training. Training in sexual matters does not require informing but rather the establishment of specific behaviors and attitudes. It will be helpful to keep this distinction in mind.

Sexual behavior can encompass a wide range of actions ranging from discussions among men and women to the sexual acts leading to orgasm. But it is when decisions are made concerning what should be said, known, or shown about the sexual organs and their use that administrators, parents, and the general public become interested. Therefore let us put aside other aspects of social behavior and consider only education and training relevant to the sexual acts, *per se*.

For all mentally deficient people whose capacities are beyond minimal levels, some form of sex education *is* being provided. Just as normal children learn from their peers and from older, bigger, and more sophisticated contemporaries, so the mentally deficient learn from their associates in the home or institution, on the job, in training programs, and on the street. Street knowledge is taken with a grain of salt by most normal teenagers. Many of the extraordinary reports and suggestions they hear about sex are rightly ascribed to the bravado of the reporter. A judgment is made on the basis of reliability, knowledge, and opportunity of the individual who is "teaching" sex on the street corner. Every report is contrasted with other reports and most treated skeptically. Furthermore, parents or teachers many times offer other information and, although information from these sources is probably treated with even greater skepticism, it does provide potential confirmation or rejection of information from other sources.

Does the mentally deficient person have the critical abilities necessary to evaluate reports from his mentors? Mentally deficient individuals are notoriously accepting of what other people tell them. And if there is no counter-balancing information from home or school, there can be nothing with which to make a comparison.

The point is that every mentally deficient person gets sex education one way or another. Sex education should not be the issue. The issue is: Should responsible institutions or agencies offer additional sex education? The second question is: Should these institutions and agencies provide training in sexual matters?

If we consider the role of institutions and agencies as providing *supplementary* training and education, almost everyone would agree that this should be done, at least as a corrective to what the mentally deficient person learns from other sources. Having reached this decision *in principle,* the practical matters of what and how much still remain.

The usual response, at this point, is to say that what is taught should be appropriate to the needs and capacities of the individual. But, this is too vague a guideline to serve any practical purpose. It also hides the moral decision about what kind of sexual activity is right for whom. This decision must be determined on the basis of the group and society in which the mentally deficient person finds himself or herself. We shall return to this matter later.

As far as information is concerned, it is easiest to drop the term sex education entirely, and only consider information regarded to *health*. What information does a mentally deficient person need to preserve and maintain his general health and well-being?

High on the list of health information would be cleanliness. The deficient person should be taught how to keep all parts of his or her body clean, including those sometimes called the private parts. They should learn when to seek medical help, the signs of vaginal infection, venereal disease, and urinary tract infection. Girls should be taught how to palpate their breasts for lumps and be convinced of the importance of seeking medical attention if abnormalities are detected. They need to be instructed in the hygenic procedures related to their monthly menstrual periods. They should also be taught the importance of periodic pelvic examinations.

The information given must be honest. It must be told straight and clearly. If the occasion arises, misinformation must be countered with appropriate facts. For example, they should learn that masturbation *per se* is not harmful physically, although certainly they should know that insertion of some objects into the vagina can be hazardous. The point is that information about health given to mentally deficient persons must be biologically and medically sound, but it also must be complete and truthful if credibility is to be maintained.

Health instruction for the mentally deficient should include information about birth control techniques, but the use of the techniques must be based on training rather than mere education. A knowlege of the fundamental process of reproduction is important for those mentally deficient people who can understand it, but specific and intensive training must also be given those who cannot.

Attitudes Toward Sex

Sexual activity in many forms is permitted in our society today. Western culture has become increasingly accepting of a variety of ways in which physical contacts and interactions occur between adults. However, our society is made up of many subcultures whose values are quite different from each other.

In any institution, the people who work with clients come from the various communities and subcultures in the area around the institution. Their backgrounds will differ and they will hold widely divergent attitudes and beliefs. Because of the divergent attitudes of these individuals, their behavior toward sexual incidents and acts will be different. And since, on a day-to-day basis, they are the authority figures, their attitudes and values about sexual conduct determine the practices of the clients they supervise. No matter what the formal or written rules for behavior may be, they are interpreted and enforced by the people working with the mentally deficient on a daily basis. As a result, the mentally deficient person may receive quite different, and often conflicting messages about sex.

Inconsistency in the attitudes and reactions about sexual matters held by people working with deficient individuals can be highly distressing to mentally deficient people. Yet these divergencies must exist because of the heterogeniety of those with whom the mentally deficient come in contact, and no amount of directives, programs, or plans issued from a central headquarters or authority will change matters. No matter how much they are urged, sexually liberal people working with the mentally deficient will not attempt to tell them that masturbation is "dirty" and forbidden. On the other hand, no sexually conservative person will endorse intercourse between institutional residents. As with most moral matters, many people think they know the right and wrong of it and will not go along with rules or programs at variance with these "true" beliefs.

The recognition of the importance of the attitudes and values of those directly concerned with clients and residents provides a different approach to the question of what sexual training *should be*. There is no absolute answer to this question. The best relative answer is one which says that the education and training should produce behaviors

137

comparable to those of nondeficient individuals in the same community.

What can be done to establish a realistic program for sexual training for the mentally deficient? Several things, provided that the importance of the attitudes of those working most closely with them is recognized. The first step is to realize that there *will* be differences of opinion.

The problem is how to merge the various attitudes of the monitors into a workable training plan. This can only be done with the development of a working plan for each living unit in the community or the institution. Consider a single unit or cottage of a large institution as a separate unit. The only way to achieve an effective sex training plan for the units is for the personnel who work on the cottage, the parents of the residents, and all other educational staff to come to a common understanding about it. This necessitates the hammering out of a group decision by all of those concerned. It may mean hours of discussion and conversation and the result may be a compromise.

These discussions among concerned parties must be frank and open. To achieve such openness may not be easy and certainly will take time. It can be done, however, and once done it will have the advantages of all decisions achieved through democratic group decisions: the support of all concerned. Yet, without achieving a group decision that all can live with, all forms of training will come to naught. One group of people will be working to weaken and counteract the goals of another.

For decisions to be made by a combined group of parents and workers, the leadership of an institution must relinquish its claims on having the final authority to design training programs and give up any claim of Solomon-like wisdom. The administrators must have confidence in the joint decisions made by employees, parents, and advocates. They must also recognize that residents, parents, and employees involved with each living unit are not interchangeable. There may well be wide differences among the units that make up a large institution or among group homes in the same geographic areas.

Factors to be Considered

In the process of decision making concerning the sexual education and training of the mentally deficient a number of issues will be considered. These are complicated matters but cannot be ignored. They all are related to the final decisions reached by the group.

139

Privacy

One of the most frequently violated "rights" of the mentally deficient person is the opportunity for privacy. All too frequently living arrangements are similar to army barracks for recruits in which rows of beds are arranged without screens or walls between them. Sexual activities are by their nature private. The physical nature of the living and recreational facilities should assure that at least some portion of everyone's life can be private.

Understanding

Sexual activities between individuals are opportunities for the sharing of love, affection, and tenderness. The extent to which a person is capable of these emotions and the extent to which these emotions are shared with others must be evaluated. Sexual activities may be little more than a handshake between friends and companionship. For a full life, opportunities should exist for friendship to be developed between men and women. This is best done under conditions in which there is freedom for men to be in contact with women and vice versa. Joint living conditions are preferable for this goal.

Consent

Few complaints are heard today about sexual activities between consenting adults.

140

Does a mentally deficient person understand enough to give meaningful consent? This is a very difficult matter, both on a practical level and for legal reasons. Even if a deficient person has been judged competent in the courts, this applies primarily to the management of money and certain business affairs. It does not mean the person would be competent to stand trial for a crime. His or her understanding of right and wrong or the more subtle aspects of a criminal act might be inadequate.

With some mentally deficient people verbal responses are very poor indicators of consent. Some tend to say yes to almost every question. They want to be accepted and liked. They have found out that yes is more likely to produce these reactions than no.

Other mentally deficient are mute or unable to speak well enough for their desires and intentions to be understood. What is to be done in such instances? People with an inability to express themselves to give consent in a meaningful way will nonetheless probably engage in some form of sexual activity. And it is silly to think that consent from a legal guardian could be obtained before every sexual act. Hence the legal approach fails us in this matter.

A more useful approach would be to ask about the kinds of problems that have led to concern over the sexual activities of the mentally deficient. In general, these are instances of pregnancy among residents of institutions, promiscuity of some residents, and rapes.

Modern medicine has made it possible to avoid unwanted pregnancies even without an on-going birth control program provided the incident is known to physicians within hours after the event and treatment given. Combining medical treatment with a method for prompt reporting of sexual intercourse can virtually assure that an unwanted child will not result. For those living outside of an institution, appropriate birth control programs should be used and indeed, the ability to use birth control programs ought to be among the necessary criteria for residential placement out in the community.

Promiscuity among mentally deficient women is another issue that comes to the attention of the public. While this is a rare occurrence (probably there is much less promiscuity among mentally deficient women than among nondeficient women of the same age and social class), the concern stems from the possibility that such women do not understand the personal nature of the sexual act, its social implications, and the possibility that they can be used by others, sometimes unknowingly, as prostitutes. The promiscuousness of mentally deficient women sometimes reflects poor preparation for community life. Neither mentally deficient boys nor girls have been trained to appreciate the meaning of intercourse as interpreted in our society. Frequently, if they have been in institutions, they have not been around people of the opposite sex for any period of time. Programs must be established, at least for the mildly deficient, that stress the extremely personal quality of sexual acts and the value of restricted sexual activity. It must be recognized, however, that a prominent feature of mental deficiency is a difficulty in appreciating rather subtle, often unspoken, social meanings. Attempts to train people to eliminate all of their sexual activity may well be more debilitating than the occasional instances of promiscuous behavior warrant.

As in all segments of society, there are mentally deficient people who gratify their sexual desires in a violent manner against the wishes of the other person. This is called rape. As mentioned before, some mentally deficient people have emotional and behavioral problems, and a few of these people take advantage of others for sexual gratification. Just as with nondeficient individuals, violent people should be isolated until their behavior is altered through acceptable training or educational programs. The mentally deficient

143

residents of an institution and the society at large must be protected from those few who relieve their sexual desires by force.

People who perform aggressive acts of any form should not be considered suitable candidates for semi- or fully-independent community living until there is reason to believe that their behavior is reasonably controlled. With the pressures for deinstitutionalization, there has been a tendency for administrators to "solve" the problem presented by a violent resident of an institution by placing that person in the community. while this solves the problem for the administrator, it fails to consider the danger that such people represent to society. It is only an expedient solution that transfers the fundamental problem to a different place.

Summary

Three types of interrelated problems were considered in this chapter: Education, emotional disturbances, and sexual practices. At the present time, the enforcement of mandatory public school education legislation seems to provide the most practical approach to securing reasonable education and training for the mentally deficient, even though it may not be the best approach *in principle*. An intensive, individual evaluation of each person's potential and actual capacities would
144

serve better, but this is not feasible at the present.

Since many mentally deficient also have emotional problems that interfere with their lives, it might be assumed that programs to alleviate this handicap would have been well studied. Such is not the case. From consideration of the handicaps of most mentally deficient, it is unlikely that either psychoanalysis or reality therapy will serve them well. One positive step would be to nurture the growth and development of each mentally deficient person. To this end a number of suggestions derived from the humanistic approach to behavior should prove most effective.

One mode of human expression is sexual activity. The different aims of sex education and training were discussed. Sex education should be based on a concern for the client's health, but training in sexual matters cannot be considered outside of the attitudes and practices of those having most direct contact with the mentally deficient. One positive step would be to develop ways in which staff and supervisory personnel could agree among themselves as to acceptable practices and acts and in that way provide a consistent approach to rules of conduct.

SIX

Steps Toward Answers

We have already found that it is not appropriate to view mentally deficient people as being perpetual children, people like us but raised in another culture, or like us but with a single tragic blemish related to learning abilities. The differences in brain structure and function must be recognized and accepted, not denied. If we must have a metaphor to describe them, let us consider them to be guests visiting us from another, yet-to-be-discovered planet.

How should we treat such visitors? We should make them welcome and offer them as much hospitality as we would hope to receive if visiting them. They have arrived without provisions and we should share ours with them, being careful not to force too much or too little on them. We should not force either our tastes or quantities on them. We should teach them about our culture, customs, and language to the extent that this can be done with their active cooperation and enjoyment. On the other hand, we should be careful not to strain their nature and goodwill. We should be careful to observe when they are happy and when they are discomforted. As good hosts, we should try to accentuate those things and events which are most pleasurable to them and minimize those which produce unhappiness.

Visiting foreign countries is always difficult. How much more difficult to visit a foreign planet! It is difficult both for the guest and for the host, especially so when the guest may be uninvited. The greatest test of a host is the ability to be kind and patient with the unexpected or uninvited guest.

By considering the mentally deficient citizens as our guests, we are in a position to examine the nature of each visitor and to design programs which provide a maximum benefit to each.

With this attitude in mind, let us turn to consider its implication for different facets of the life of the mentally deficient, in particular, the matter of human rights and values.

The Goals of the Programs

The aim of programs for the mentally handicapped should be to provide those conditions and circumstances that are most conducive to their happiness and personal growth. Programs of education and vocational training should be supportive of these goals rather than be ends in themselves. To place happiness and growth as top priority goals is to change from a work-oriented ethic to one based on human satisfactions. In a very real sense, this is a revolutionary attitude.

It will immediately be argued that happiness and personal growth are wonderful goals for all people but that these are not the *right* of anyone. Why should the dull-witted be cared for at the expense of unhappy, work-burdened, troubled citizens without mental deficiency? Frankly, there is no answer to this question except to say that they are appropriate goals for everyone and that our society ought to move toward making them attainable for as many as possible. Perhaps the plans developed for the mentally deficient could become models for the development of better lives for all.

Movements toward Growth and Happiness as a Right

Even in some of the most dehumanizing lines of work, such as industries with massive production lines, unions and management are working to establish new degrees of freedom of choice of jobs, changes in assignments, and in other conditions that allow for a more complete human development in work.

Most societies have determined that no one should starve, live in squalor, or be deprived of health care or education because of a lack of money. Our society is moving toward goals related to increased personal development. This is possible, of course, because our society is rich enough to provide the necessary housing, food, education, and health services for people even though some do not actively contribute to the products and services of the total group. Despite the many faults of our welfare systems, they do exist and are accepted, in principle, by society. A return to more primitive and harsher treatment of the poor and disabled is neither politically nor philosophically possible.

Beyond the purely physical maintenance of the mentally deficient, the philosophical basis for their treatment should be the *acceptance of them as they are and not how we would like them to be.* Accepting them must include accepting their limited potential for accomplishment.

Institutions

Institutions are needed for the mentally deficient and they will continue to be needed. In the first place, most residents of such institutions are profoundly and severely retarded and there is no other way to care for them. Many suffer from multiple handicaps, such as blindness, deafness, cerebral palsy, and epilepsy along with mental deficiency. In most states, institutions have relatively few mildly or moderately retarded that do not have other types of problems. This is an important fact that is too often ignored in the discussion of institutions.

The majority of people would agree that for such heavily handicapped people there are no alternatives to institutional care. The only contrary opinion might be those who might suggest that these greatly affected people be killed since they are an unnecessary burden to the rest of us. This opinion is so far removed from the values of our society that it scarcely needs discussion. With rare exceptions citizens of our society endorse the role of institutions for the severely and profoundly deficient. Most would further agree that their lives should be made as pleasant as possible given their restricted abilities.

Therefore, let us be done with all extreme views about the abolition of institutions for the mentally deficient. Let us consider instead what these institutions should be like.

The institutional care for the profoundly deficient and those with related physical handicaps should be directed toward making life as pleasant as possible. Basically, this amounts to nutritious food, comfortable circumstances, opportunities to be in contact with others, and a large amount of sensitive, loving care. However, caring for the physical comforts of the profoundly deficient is only the first step. Concern over their personal growth must be expressed, as well. One of the important features here is communication with other people.

Earlier (pp. 118-19), we saw the remarkable advances in behavior and communication made by profoundly retarded people with extreme forms of cerebral palsy who were allowed to interact with each other for the first time. This was done by letting the individuals make visual and tactual contact with others with similar problems. Contact with other people is essential to a satisfying life. This is a most difficult matter for the severely handicapped just in terms of physical arrangements, but with a creative approach much more can be done than is now being done. The care of the profoundly deficient requires creative management by cottage personnel, close observation by nurses, good medical treatment, including specialists in orthopedic problems, and an attitude that constantly seeks new ideas for how the life of a particular person can be enriched.

One important reason for the relative neglect of institutions for the mentally deficient has been the hopeless condition of so many of the residents. Especially depressing are those with the greatest deficiencies. There are no cures for them. There is no bright side of the coin. Because of the permanency of the mental and physical conditions, our action-oriented attitudes have not made the improvements of the conditions of the profoundly deficient a high priority goal. Rehabilitation programs are not created for them because it is so apparent that they will not ever become contributors to society. Without prospects of becoming a contributor, they are left to survive, to be warehoused and stored until they die.

Historically, institutions for the mentally deficient have been based on medical (hospital) or warehouse models. Their main thrust has been custodial with physician-administrators acting mainly as the gatekeepers.

In most institutions the mildly and moderately deficient receive the greatest attention, the most programs and treatments. The severely and profoundly deficient are relegated to the back wards, well off the main pathways of visitors. The greater the handicap, the greater the crowding and more barren the environment. The less the handicap, the smaller the living group and the better the conditions. This general procedure is rationalized on the basis that it is more efficient to deal with the most incapacitated in an assembly-line fashion and the related belief that those least handicapped can profit most from "nice conditions and better programs." There may also be the implicit view that the least handicapped are closest to "being human."

What groups or types of individuals should be given special attention? The answer is none. Every person is capable of greater growth and happiness. The profoundly deficient person deserves as much opportunity for happiness as the mildly deficient. Growth in skills or abilities may be slow and apparently minor in the profoundly deficient, but their subjective feelings of accomplishment and happiness may be as great or greater than those of people with less of a handicap. How important would it be for a profoundly retarded person to establish a first contact with another human being? What is the degree of joy experienced when such a person learns to feed himself? Is it any more or less rewarding than when a moderately deficient person learns to read a few words?

The awarding of special consideration and attention to the least deficient individuals is sometimes justified on the basis that this will allow them to be prepared for placement in the community, usually in a group or foster home. The ultimate goal is for them to leave the group or foster home to be absorbed by society at large. It is presumed that the additional attention will pay off when they find employment, become tax-payers, and lead "normal" lives. The entire focus is to prepare them for life in the "real" world outside the institution. For those with moderate degrees of deficiencies the goals remain the same, even when it is clear that they will be unable to find or hold employment on a competitive basis. The argument is that these mentally deficient will be in sheltered workshops which can provide the means for a semi-independent life.

Life on the Outside

The examination of the lives of the mentally deficient living outside institutions indicates that they do not have a great deal of success. They tend to take jobs shunned by others. The rates of pay are below the average for the type of work they do. Often they must take temporary positions of a menial nature. They are the first to be laid off when the job market becomes tight. They are not, and generally cannot become, qualified for advancement. Because of the nature of their deficiencies they usually find it impossible to profit from most job-training and job-improvement programs. They find it difficult or impossible to plan for the future, including making plans for health care, insurance, and retirement.

For those unable to be competitive in the job market, and this includes the majority of the mentally deficient, the opportunity to survive by employment in a sheltered workshop is often an illusion. Very few cities and even fewer rural areas have been able to establish and maintain such programs. To be sure there are a few successful programs scattered about the country, but these are the exceptions rather than the rule. Often young and middle-aged adults report to the sheltered workshop to find no regular work and no regime for job training. They wind up sitting around bored or horsing around with the other clients. Matching the little or no training and little or no work, there is little or no compensation. Plans for the future of sheltered workshops are always rosy and hopeful. Seldom do these plans ever reach fulfillment.

Therefore, there is no way in which a person with less than the capacity for full employment to achieve even minimal living standards. Unfortunately, plans for a meaningful life for the moderately deficient based on community based workshops are illusory.

Even for those mildly deficient capable of full employment, life is not possible without regular supervision and guidance. Mentally deficient people who survive in the community do so only by dependence on the support of others whether they be chance acquaintances, neighbors, or paid social workers.

The mentally deficient individuals need help and guidance. Information and direction are essential to them. Under ideal circumstances, this advice and guidance would always be useful and appropriate. However, mentally deficient individuals are besieged by information and advice from several sources about all types of problems. They get advice whether it is asked for or not. Sometimes this advice is helpful, but at other times it is erroneous and leads the individual into difficulties.

To some extent everyone needs advice, counsel, and direction. We seek help in understanding the complexities of the income tax report forms, about health insurance, Social Security benefits, and other federal and state assistance. Usually, when the nondeficient person seeks advice, sources are selected on the basis of past experience or informed knowledge. Advisors are carefully selected. Unsolicited advice is most carefully evaluated. However, the mentally deficient individual usually does not select appropriate sources or carefully evaluate the competency of the advisor.

There are a number of reasons for this. One of these is that the mentally deficient individual is often struggling for social acceptance. Many mentally handicapped people want to make friends and be accepted by others. Related to this desire for social acceptance is the attempt to hide limited intellectual abilities. One of the strongest desires of all mentally deficient individuals is to be seen as "normal." The mentally deficient individual often believes that to reject advice might lead to rejection by the advisor.

Another aspect of the willingness of the mentally deficient individual to accept advice without critical evaluations is a lessened ability to delay action. As has been mentioned before, many mentally deficient individuals have trouble withholding actions. The easiest and quickest solution to a problem is often accepted. If the advice given seems to represent a quick solution to what seems to be a difficult problem, it may well be accepted simply because it is action.

For these, and perhaps other reasons, the evaluation of advice by mentally handicapped people is inadequate. Some examples of these difficulties may be in order. There was, for instance, a mentally deficient individual who had been told many times that he was diabetic and must maintain a strict, low sugar diet. However, he could not refuse gifts of candy or other sugarfilled desserts. When urged to "go ahead, it won't hurt you," he did. Sometimes these well-wishers who urged the mentally deficient person to accept the delicacy were well-intentioned, but the result was nonetheless dangerous, and frequently led to diabetic coma and shock. As another example, mentally deficient people are often given advice on income tax matters. Sometimes the advice is bad, as when a person was told in jest, that there was no need to fill out the forms since the government already had his money. Sometimes retarded individuals have been told to accept whatever pay is offered for any type of job because they will be sent back to the institution or even to jail if they do not.

Another real problem for the mentally deficient is buying merchandise over the telephone or from door-to-door salesmen. They are easy prey to unscrupulous peddlers of mythical awards and opportunities that lead to the purchase of many expensive items on time-payment plans. The mentally deficient individual may buy products, often the same one repeatedly, for which they have no need or use.

In the hope of preparing individuals for independent life, much attention is given to communicative skills, job-training, and living skills, but very little is given to understanding the importance of resisting the overtures of salesmen and the evaluation of advice. Nondeficient people do not accept advice without question. Advice from different sources is sought before a decision is made. Lacking skepticism, mentally deficient people are at the mercy of any unscrupulous person who happens along.

The Paradox of Community Living

Despite the uncomfortable living conditions of most mentally deficient with moderate abilities, their poor employment prospects, and other disadvantages, they consistently report a strong desire to remain in the community rather than return to an institution. The paradox is that physical conditions of life are often better in the institution than on the streets. Why should they wish to remain in unfavorable circumstances in the community rather than return to the safe grounds of the institution?

One reason is that the quality of life in most institutions is only marginally better than the lowest level of life outside. Food is poorly prepared, served in an unappetizing fashion in large cafeteria-style halls, and is available only on a rigid schedule designed to meet the convenience of the staff. Housing conditions may resemble those of an Army barracks. Educational, vocational, and recreational programs may be nonexistent. Boredom is the only thing that fills the day. With such conditions, the choice between the two is clear: pick the community with all of its troubles and discomforts.

However, even if the food were good, the living conditions decent, and the day occupied with work or school in institutions, the community offers another precious commodity, freedom. The freedom to come and go, the freedom to eat when one wants to, the freedom to be energetic or lazy. Freedom of all kinds and descriptions.

Institutions by their nature are places of routine, orderliness, and rigid schedules. It is easier to handle large numbers of people if they all do the same thing at the same time. It is efficient to be orderly, or so it seems. Regimentation is a frequent consequence of the desire for efficiency.

The typical day at an institution begins at an early hour when residents are told to "rise and shine." The next steps include the bathroom, dressing, and making the beds. Cleaning the cottage or work follows, usually before breakfast. Often this requires a march through the grounds to the dining hall. Then the day begins at seven or eight AM. Some go to school, some to work, some do nothing except wander the grounds. Whatever they do, they cannot mess up the cottage or lie in the freshly made beds. The lunch line forms early. So does the dinner line. After dinner, television can be watched for a while. Then it is time to wash and go to bed at eight or nine PM. One day follows the next in a gray progression without noticeable change. It is little wonder that people do not want to return to such conditions.

We should note, however, that there are some individuals for whom freedom is not a blessing but a curse. Some mentally deficient individuals who have tried community living find that the uncertainties of society are too much to handle. They wish to be returned to institutional care. Not only is community life too complex for them but they do not like the way they are treated by the outsiders with whom they come in contact. For them, it is easier to accept the institution. The situation is not dissimilar to that found with some habitual criminals who, when released from prisons, actively seek ways to be returned. For them, also, the world is too hostile and unfriendly. The responsibilities associated with freedom can be a heavy burden.

Everyone wants to be treated as a person of value, to be respected, to be accepted. Many mentally deficient people do not experience such treatment because they are regarded as insignificant by others around them. Even worse, they are often treated as fools and made fun of. Insults can be expressed in many ways, not the least of which is when the mentally deficient are simply ignored. They are talked about by people around them as if they were invisible. Perhaps the nondeficient people who do this do not believe the mentally deficient understand or care, but they do.

The mentally deficient person has many other problems in even casual interactions with others. These include being unable to talk about events of the day which are printed in newspapers they cannot read, difficulties in talking about any abstract idea or concept, problems in evaluating and counting money, telling time, and even in simple neighborhood sporting events in which their lack of coordination makes them bystanders rather than participants. It is only natural that many prefer the company of others with similar mental handicaps to the unkind or thoughtless actions of some nondeficient people.

Freedom in the Institutions

Freedom and dignity can exist in institutions. In principle, there is no reason why an institution cannot be made into a small community with freedom offered to residents to the extent it is desired and can be accepted. Within this community there would be different degrees of responsibilities as well as freedoms. A person should be able to select the most appropriate degree of freedom and the responsibilities associated with it. Furthermore, these freedoms and responsibilities could serve as incentives to lead the person to consider the possibility of independent or semi-independent life outside of the institution.

Let us first consider living conditions. Within an institution, apartments and group living homes could be established that are similar to those found outside the walls. People who live in them could pay rent, utilities, and telephone bills just as they would on the outside. The only differences would be that these would be within the institution and subject to periodic examination by officials of the institution. Group living homes could also be made available within the institution and the mentally deficient person could live in them with other similarly handicapped individuals just as they would do in group living homes outside the institutions. The group living situations in institutions could provide different degrees of freedom. Some would be highly supervised with a great deal of care provided. Others would be minimally supervised and most of the services provided by the residents, themselves. A choice of living conditions would be allowed and no one pushed to a greater amount of freedom than the person wants or is able to handle.

The ability of the individual to choose a less restrictive living situation would also be dependent on the willingness of the individual to accept responsibility. The right to live in less restrictive circumstances must be coupled with responsibility and reasonable patterns of behavior in regard to other people and property.

What is called for is a progressive series of living arrangements in which fewer and fewer restrictions are placed upon the individual's freedom. In an apartment situation the individual would have privacy and opportunity to live almost as he or she sees fit. The right to this independent life would be earned through work and contributions to the lives of others within the institution. It should also be possible for people to work in the community and to live in group living units or apartments within the institution either on a permanent basis or as a transition to living in the community. Such an arrangement should heighten interest in educational and vocational programs since they would lead toward both better employment opportunities and increased freedom. These opportunities should be available both within the institution and on the outside. Greater freedom of living would provide obvious goals for many residents in an institution. The value of preparing oneself for educational and vocational advancement would be clear and unequivocal.

By contrast, in institutions today residents go to schools or vocational training programs, but often they can see no immediate benefits from the programs. There are promises, of course, that he may someday be able to go to the "outside." What does the "outside" mean to the mentally deficient person? By having the group homes and the apartments inside the institution, a gradual transition could be made. The outside world could be seen more realistically and a choice made about how much of it was wanted or needed.

For those in apartments, the right to prepare food and snacks whenever they are wanted would be possible. The choice of foods in the group living homes could be based on the degree of self-sufficiency in the group. The greater the capabilities and desires of the people, the more freedom would be allowed in moving around the grounds and off the institution.

Work with Choice

One of the first objections to the proposal for a greater diversity in living conditions in institutions is that there are not enough opportunities for residents to earn sufficient money to allow them to pay for their group homes or apartments. However, even if the cost of these living quarters were entirely subsidized, the overall cost would be less than if they were in standard living units with the usual amount of supervision. The greatest proportion of the cost of institutions is in the people needed for direct care and supervision. But, it should also be recognized that steps could be taken to increase the financial contribution of the mentally deficient through employment on the grounds of institutions. Very little attempt has been made to stimulate the development of private light industries actually on the grounds of institutions. This could be encouraged in a number of ways, such as the leasing of land or public buildings at low rates. The amount of reduction in rental fees for the use of the land or building could be made on the basis of the number of mentally deficient people to be employed by the industry. Furthermore, most mentally deficient people have an adjusted rate of base pay established through procedures monitored by the federal government to reflect their relative work capacities. This could make them desirable employees for industry.

It is also obvious that many types of skills could be used by residents to improve their personal conditions and those of the institutions. These include those related to farming, nursery operations, and custodial duties. Furthermore, individuals with special musical, artistic, or other abilities should be encouraged to develop them on the same basis that they are encouraged by society at large. Those who entertain and beautify, for example, should be supported and encouraged for their efforts. Systems could be established whereby those with special abilities could be rewarded within the institutional framework by greater freedom and less supervised living conditions. Such rewards need not be done entirely by judgments made by staff or administrators but should include judgments made by the residents.

These proposals may seem to be like the token economies which have been established in certain institutions on an experimental basis for some time. In such economies people do different tasks or behave in different ways to obtain tokens (poker chips, special currencies, or something similar) that can be exchanged for various benefits and rewards. The suggestion made here differs from token economies in that there is nothing token about it. It is calling for the establishment of a real economy based on living conditions and responsibilities.

There are many additional advantages in the establishment of apartments and group living homes with various degrees of supervision on the grounds of institutions. Not the least of these, is that they would provide a training experience for people who want to work in group homes in the community and for social workers who will be visiting mentally deficient people in all types of circumstances. Living in the less restrictive group homes within the institution would be a tentative step toward group home living in the community.

The present suggestion is firmly based on freedom of choice. Basic life supports, reasonable food, and decent living conditions would be provided to everyone. A person could search out and test the degree of freedom and responsibility that is most satisfying. In addition, the absolute amount of income received by a person need not be related to their living circumstances. Presumably, a full work load would be one of the prerequisites for independent apartment living. However, because of the different vocational rating scales established for different degrees of mental and physical impairments, the amount of compensation could vary. For example, if a person works maximally and had a vocational efficiency rating of thirty percent, his or her wage would be less than that received by a person working maximally at an efficiency ratio of seventy percent. The requirements for entering the less restrictive living conditions ought to be a maximal effort at whatever the person's vocational efficiency rating is. Even though financial contributions would be different, the consequences in terms of living conditions would be the same. And as a person

170

enters into the less restrictive living conditions, other demands would be made. These include reasonable social behavior and cooperation with their peers. Reasonable care of their furniture and surroundings would also be required. Aggressive actions toward others, destruction of property, or poor personal cleanliness would result in a loss of privileges and a return to more closely supervised living conditions.

Community Programs

Living conditions outside of institutions should also have different degrees of freedom and supervision. If a variety of living conditions can be established within institutions, then transitions could easily be made to similar conditions in the community. For example, a person who has demonstrated the ability to live in a minimally supervised apartment situation on the grounds of an institution could try independent living in the community. While this graded series would overlap with some of the living situations found in the institutions, it would also differ from the institutional programs in that there would be fewer highly supervised living units and, for a very few, there would be the possibility for totally independent existence. (It must not be forgotten that the complete freedom through independent living in the com-

171

munity will not be possible for most mentally deficient people.)

In so far as possible, the mentally deficient people should have the right to decide their own levels of independence. It should not be a decision made by someone else on the basis of its being good for them. People should be able to make decisions about the degree of freedom in their own living conditions on the basis of previously acquired experience and knowledge. For those who cannot make such decisions in a competent fashion it should be made by legal guardians or parents in conjunction with others who have knowledge of the individual's abilities *and* desires.

All-or-None
Transfers to the Community

All too frequently mentally deficient people are abruptly placed in a group or foster home with minimal supervision and programs. They are placed in the community as a one-time, one-way transfer out of the institution. From then on, the person is expected to survive with little or no supervision.

This emergence is often a sudden shock and one for which the person is ill-prepared. Attempts to reduce the magnitude of the shock usually take the form of educational, vocational, and recreational programs in the institution but too often there is little experience with independence before the transfer is made. Another related problem is that the amount of supervision available in the community is the same for all group and foster homes. Programs for all are directed toward employment and independent living despite the impossibility of attaining this goal for most of the mentally deficient. The choice is limited to two alternatives: being in the institution or out. What is called for is the development of options of life-style both in the institution and in the community.

A Right to Retreat

In the series of supervised experiences available in the institution, a person would be able to move back from a situation that has too little supervision to one with greater structure or to ones with different living conditions. A similar situation should be available to the person living in the community. Everyone should be encouraged to move toward or away from structured situations according to their own feelings and needs. This should include the ability to indicate a desire to go back to an institution or to a group home situation. Unfortunately, it is often the case that mentally deficient people are forced to go out into the community. The way back to a more protective environment is difficult or impossible, even if the person

173

loses a job, completes a vocational program without being able to find employment, or becomes physically or mentally ill.

Locations of Community Living Units
When institutions for the feebleminded were first established, they were located in rural areas far from the disturbing hustle and bustle of cities. They were institutions built on the goal of putting the mentally deficient into more-or-less productive labor of an agricultural sort, removing them from urban confusion, and hiding the residents from public view. They were also seen as the means whereby the general public could be protected from the unpredictable actions of the residents.

This philosophy is still reflected today in the establishment of group and foster homes in predominantly agricultural areas, a tendency now reinforced by economic considerations. However, there is a significant difference between the establishment of reasonably large institutions and isolated foster or group homes in similar areas. Institutions of some size have the financial means to employ specialists in vocational and physical therapy, educators, physicians, dentists, and the like. Furthermore, there were many residents with rather similar handicaps. When a few clients are placed in isolated rural

174

circumstances, few, if any, of these important services are available. All too frequently, people are simply placed in a rural home away from jobs, public transportation, public schools, and vocational training facilities. Recently some groups have argued against placing people in rural group or foster homes because they will usually be deprived of programs and services and will not be able to learn about the normal experiences to be found primarily in urban settings. Jobs, education, and training will not be those representative of the lives led by most Americans. There is some basis to this argument; the mentally deficient living in isolated rural areas usually do not have rich programs, good services, or the opportunity for a wide selection among jobs or job-training programs. However, the placement of the mentally deficient in urban settings has great difficulties as well.

City-Living: The Future

One of the great problems faced by the United States is that of the large cities. It is in New York, Los Angeles, Chicago, Detroit, and the like that the stress of unemployment, inflation, and urban disintegration are most keenly felt. It is the great cities that have the largest proportions of people on welfare, about 18% in some cases. In some cities there

175

soon will be three generations of people who *never* have had employment.

Are these congested, nearly bankrupt cities appropriate places for the mentally deficient to be "normalized"? Is it appropriate for the mentally deficient to be placed in conditions where there is mass unemployment and where they would have to compete with those already out of work? Should they be "normalized" into the welfare-dependent groups of the poverty stricken inner cities? Should they become a new, lowest layer in the urban struggle for existence?

It is doubtful that most readers would feel that group and foster living homes ought to be established in the heart of urban slums even if they are the normal experience for a substantial segment of the urban society. Most people would reject this argument because they share the philosophy advocated earlier in this chapter: that the mentally deficient are like guests of our society, unwilling visitors to our strange land. Most people would agree that there is a collective responsibility for protecting and helping these "visitors."

Therefore, the concept of normalization does not provide adequate guidance for the establishment of programs in the community. What is needed is a principle that would justify working toward establishing conditions that would allow the mentally deficient to live as full an existence as possible. One principle is not hard to understand, since it is based on human kindness and concern for those who are unable to help themselves. A name for the principle is love.

Given such a principle, where would be the best places to establish group or foster homes? They should be where the conditions of happiness and personal growth could be achieved. They could be in the urban complex, near to established educational, vocational, and health services, but only for people for whom a productive life is possible and desired. For other people with different interests and abilities, the city with its perils and troubles may not be appropriate.

Because of the changing character of American life and the changes occurring throughout the industrialized Western World, the nature of programs for the mentally deficient must change. The key to the future is not in the abolition of institutions in favor of community life, but rather in terms of expanded alternatives for varying degrees of freedom and supervision in both institutions and the community. The walls of institutions should not crumble but become permeable so that people can move through them in both directions when conditions dictate. The institutions must extend into the community and the community into the institution.

Economic Considerations

It could be argued that the proposed plans for increasing the number of alternative forms of living in institutions and outside of them would be desirable but not feasible economically. But, their implementation would cost no more than is now being spent on the mentally deficient. In apartments and less restrictive group living homes the clients would be supervised only on a periodic basis. This would mean a reduction in the number of cottage life and supervisory personnel needed.

In addition, the present plan calls for financial payments to the state by clients who are working on the grounds, or off grounds, toward their supervision, food and housing. The amount contributed by the residents from their work would be adjusted on the basis of the degree of vocational debilitation and the net proceeds from their efforts. Formulas for the proportionment of resident-earned income to the state and the individual have been developed by most states already. The greater encouragement of industrial or business enterprises on grounds would create income to the institution in the form of rent that would offset the cost of creating the group homes and apartment complexes. An additional savings could be obtained through the use of these group living homes and the apartments for the training of cottage personnel, group home operators, and social workers.

Less obvious savings would be made in the reduction of money spent outside the institutions in the form of rent to private parties or group living homes. When a state contracts for group or foster homes, it is also enhancing the value of the property and furnishings, and paying the principal on the mortgage, but not receiving any equity in the property. By having some of the group homes and apartments owned by the state these financial advantages would accrue to the public instead of to private individuals. All in all, it is likely that the proposal would result in a financial savings to the state as well as to the improvement of the conditions of the mentally deficient.

The total financial impact of a single mentally deficient person can be estimated more or less exactly. If institutional care for a mentally deficient person is estimated to be $12,000 per year and the life expectancy is about 50 years, the total cost to a state would be $600,000 over the life of the mentally deficient person. Anything that helps that person contribute to his or her own maintenance obviously helps to reduce that burden to the state.

While these proposals for progressive, less restrictive conditions for mentally deficient adults could lower the cost of care, the only way that the total amount spent will be greatly reduced will be through the reduction of the frequency of mental deficiencies. This can be done only by applying basic knowledge about brain development and brain damage to the developing child. It may well be that some day it will be possible to stimulate new cell growth in order to replace cells lost or not formed as a consequence of damage to the developing brain. Chemical intervention with the developing fetus could prevent malformation of the brain after injury by suppressing the formation of aberrant systems and fiber tracts. Genetic counseling and prenatal discovery of developmental problems could lead to a reduction in the numbers of the mentally defective children as well as providing better prenatal care to mothers. Nevertheless, there will be some people with brains that have developed in unusual ways and to them we must extend the hand of welcome to our society.

Summary

The basis of the proposals in this chapter is a change in the approach used to consider the mentally deficient in our society. They should be considered as our guests. As a result, we should strive to make their lives happier and more fulfilling, rather than concentrate only on how to make them productive.

To do this a major reorganization of living conditions in the community and in institutions is required. *Both* must offer a variety of conditions from which the mentally deficient person can elect different degrees of freedom and responsibility. The mentally deficient person must be able to earn freedom of action through his or her own efforts, but this should not be evaluated only on the basis of the monetary value of his labor. Each person's special contributions must be valued and appreciated.

The freedom of choice must be a paramount consideration. This must include the ability to choose less restrictive living circumstances or more restrictive circumstances as befits the individual's current needs and capacities. Choices must include a return to institutional life as well as the move away from it. There must be freedom to move back and forth from the institution to the community as is necessary for employment and for appropriate living conditions. The walls of the institution must be permeable.

The concept of normalization must be reconsidered in spirit of love and charity. The placement of group and foster living homes into rural and urban settings must be re-evaluated in light of current needs and conditions. The issue should be where would our guest be must adequately sustained rather than what would be the closest approach to a normal life.

The proposals of this chapter probably would cost no more than present programs and, if coupled with greater business activity within institutions, could even cost less. The main consideration, however, would be that their implementation would lead to richer and fuller lives for all of our mentally deficient fellow citizens.